WORDS ABOUT WHITEINCH
A Celebration of Local Identity

Edited by Joyce Ito and Sarah Ward
Illustrated by Annabel Wright
Designed and set by Edwin Pickstone

Typeset in Sh Perpetua

Printed, on Munken, and bound in Scotland by Montgomery Litho Group

Copyright 2010 Whiteinch Centre Press

First published in January 2010 by
Whiteinch Centre Press
Whiteinch Centre Limited
1 Northinch Court
Glasgow
G14 0UG

ISBN: 978-0-9564945-0-4

The publishers acknowledge funding from
Awards for All
Scottish Government Wider Role
Glasgow City Council Area Committee Fund

FORWARD

When I was asked to write something for Words about Whiteinch,
I said, Aye! straight away. For a start, Whiteinch is an area of Glasgow dear
to my heart. I've spent many a braw afternoon there having coffee with
friends and gabbing till my jaws were sore (a mean feat for me!) but I get
the feeling that Whiteinch is more than just a chat-stop... there's a real sense
of community there which is sadly on the wane, not just in Glasgow but
nationally. Almost everyone's hooked on some kind of insular technology:
pc, xbox, mobile...Whiteinch is an example of the wee corner of humanity
still left in us when we meet eye to eye and work hand in hand. To have a
book of stories that reflect and celebrate this rarity is something I'm not
only glad to be involved in, but also grateful to be touched by.

Karen Dunbar

ACKNOWLEDGEMENTS

The editors would like to show our gratitude to the following people and organisations for their valuable contribution to Words about Whiteinch:

Thanks to Etta Dunn, Kathrine Sowerby and Whiteinch Primary School for their contribution to local creative writing workshops, and to all workshop participants for making the workshops a fun and enriching experience.

Thanks to all those who contributed to the text: all the local writers who submitted their work; friends and colleagues who contributed including Carl McDougall, Sam Greene, Etta Dunn, Neil McKay and Barry Docherty; and thanks to Professor Tom Leonard for contributing work by poet Marion Bernstein.

Thanks to Michael Schmidt for his most valuable support with the editorial process, and to Edwin Pickstone and Annabel Wright for their patience and expertise with the design and illustration respectively.

Thanks to Whiteinch Centre Limited for supporting the project, and, last but not least, thanks to our funders at Awards for All, Glasgow City Council Area Committee and Scottish Government Wider Role for funding workshops, publications and launch costs. We are grateful that they have been willing to pledge their commitment to celebrating local identity through creative writing.

Joyce Ito and Sarah Ward

CONTENTS

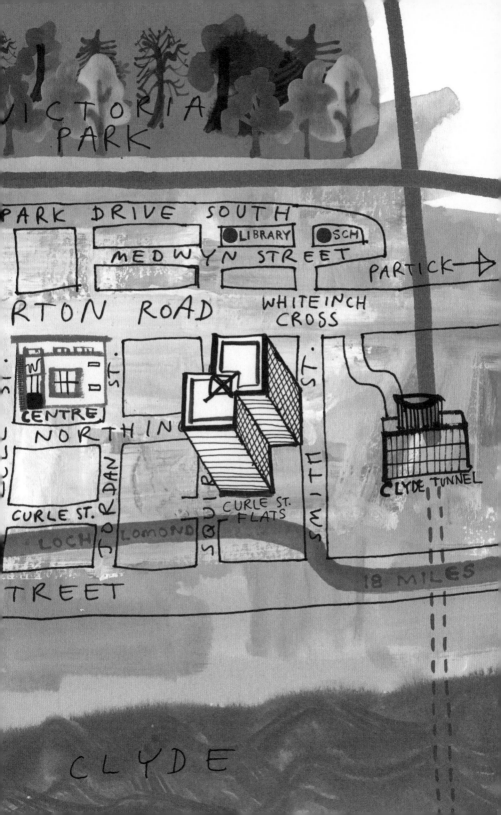

1: Whiteinch Cross

LAST YEAR
Lauren Skoglund (age 9)

Last Year, I saw Whiteinch moving
Cars ran down the street
past angry houses
Buses chased the cars
but had to catch their breath
Giant horses stood higher than houses
Flats tried to walk over me
but they were too stiff
The trees hair was blowing in the wind
Balconies clung to buildings
for their life
The pond cuddled me with its watery arms
The shows spun round and round
until they felt dizzy
The telephone box swallowed me up.

THE TUNNEL
Sam Greene

Samuel Greene was born in 1935 in Glenties, County Donegal in the Irish Republic. His mum, Madge, worked in the railway gatehouse; his dad, Con, was a plate layer, responsible for laying railway line and carrying out maintenance and repairs between Glenties and Finntown. Con Greene was promoted to stationmaster at Finntown and the family moved to the station house. It was an isolated place but Sammy had sisters and brothers and they had the countryside for a playground.

Finntown station closed in 1948 leaving the family homeless and Con unemployed. When Sammy was thirteen, the family boarded the Laird's Lough at Derry to sail to a new life in Glasgow. It was a big adventure. The boatmen unloaded the cattle at Whiteinch and then they sailed on to the Broomielaw where all the Irish folk poured off in search of work. Sammy's Daddy and his two big brothers, Connie and Michael, went away to Loch Awe to work on a railway tunnel. His big sister, Isobel, got a job as a live-in housekeeper for a doctor in Queen's Park. Sammy, Neil, Mary and their mum stayed in two rooms rented from Mrs Doherty in Balvicar St near Queens Park.

Sammy was sent for milk on the first morning in the big city; he watched the trams and wondered how on earth they stayed on the lines: he'd never seen tramlines sunk into the road before and thought it must be some fabulous Glaswegian engineering. Mrs. Doherty took him to the cinema at Victoria Road and Sammy loved it even though the screen shook every time the train passed.

When Sammy's Dad and the older boys had saved up enough money for a deposit the family moved into their own home in Paisley Road West. From his window Sammy could watch the flood of men pouring into the shipyards; when his cousin Sheila visited from Ireland she thought it was a funeral procession. She woke Sammy up to ask who'd died that so many people were there. It was the only time she'd seen such a big crowd.

Sammy loved growing up in Glasgow though he hated school and left

as soon as he could. Jobs were easy to find and he worked at all sorts though his favourite was in the cinema operating the reels, where he could watch all the films for free. He revelled in the excitement of the city, loved the dance-halls and the Italian cafes, though he thought spaghetti was the most revolting stuff he'd ever seen and refused to put a single worm of it in his mouth!

Sam was a married man and Daddy to his first child, Kathleen, when his father's long experience of tunnels and railways landed him the job of foreman for the new Clyde Tunnel at Whiteinch. Con Greene was in charge of operations outside the tunnel and responsible for the construction and maintenance of the railway line that was used to take the men and tools back and forth and collect the tons of debris to be removed to the surface. As was common in those days, Con recruited his workforce from men he knew were capable and reliable including his three sons and his two sons-in-law. About half the tunnel workforce was Irish. All the men had to undergo a medical examination to ensure they were fit to work underground at the thirty two pounds per square inch of pressure present under all those tons of water. The doctor discovered Sam had a heart murmur and barred him from working underground; he was given the job of lock keeper.

When the technical work was complete a dozen men armed with drills, pneumatic tools and jackhammers began to dig the first shaft at the Govan end in July 1957. A huge machine called The Shield, originally designed by Marc Brunel (father of Isambard) for the Thames tunnel was then lowered in and assembled. The front end of The Shield was divided into sixteen cells: each cell had a space for one miner digging with a pickaxe or pneumatic drill. The miners stood on platforms: in front of them were planks of wood holding back the soil. They would unscrew one plank and remove eighteen inches of soil from behind it, replace that plank further forward, then unscrew the next plank and do the same. Eventually all the planks had shifted by eighteen inches at which point the whole tunnel shield was moved forward by pistons. A cast iron circle in some eight pieces was then bolted into the new space. It was a slow process at best and the going varied from thirty feet a week for soft brown clay to as little as nine feet a week for boulder clay.

One night the men were making slow progress, and decided to go forty inches instead of the usual eighteen; the mistake caused a collapse that killed three miners. The men waited at the top to discover the identity of the dead and Sam was never so glad to see his brother, Michael, emerge from underground.

The tunnel was a dangerous place. To stop water coming in as they dug, the air pressure in the digging chamber was increased using compressors. The air pressure inside the tunnel had to be higher than the pressure outside, to stop water and gravel coming in. One day the compressed air found its way out; a fountain could be seen coming out of the Clyde. The men were paid triple time round the clock to plug the leak and prevent collapse. Hundreds of tons of puddle clay were poured in to plug the gap from the outside. A hundred bales of straw were taken into the tunnel and used to stop the gap from the inside. This held the leak at bay until tons of concrete could be poured in. The puddle clay then had to be removed, though the bales of straw are still there embedded in the concrete.

The lock keeper's job was to operate the decompression chamber to ensure that men coming up did not suffer the bends. Just like divers, men who had been working in the tunnel would have nitrogen from the air dissolved in the water in their body. This is similar to the way pressurised carbon dioxide dissolves in water to make fizzy drinks. If a tunneller was brought to the surface too quickly then his body would fill with bubbles of nitrogen gas. The result is an extremely painful and potentially fatal condition called 'the bends' or decompression sickness. The time required for decompression depended on the time underground, but normally took more than an hour. There was another shaft called the 'muck shaft' that was used to bring up dirt and tools, anything that wasn't human; Sam suspected men would sneak into the muck tunnel to save decompression time. They didn't seem to understand their lives were at risk. The men were instructed to be very careful to report any feelings of illness. Local people were alerted that men staggering like drunks could be suffering from decompression sickness and not just too many pints. Over the time of the tunnel's construction four hundred and sixty nine men had to be treated for the bends; seventy one cases were serious, and two men died.

The Clyde Tunnel took seven years to build, with completion in March 1964. In planning it was estimated that the tunnel would take nine thousand vehicles daily, but by 2005 there were sixty five thousand vehicles passing through.

Sam Greene lives in the village of Milford, County Donegal, sixty kilometres from Finntown where his father was Station Master. His son, Sam, lives nearby with his wife and three kids. Sam adores living in the countryside of his beloved Ireland, but returns to Glasgow regularly to visit Kathleen and Fran, his daughter and son in law and their four children. When the kids were wee they used to have a competition to see who could hold their breath for the drive through and Sammy would tell them all about how their family helped to build the Clyde Tunnel.

WHITEINCH IN FLIGHT
Alistair Bain

James looked up at the ships clearing the airspace above Whiteinch. Those vessels couldn't go with them, he thought sadly, but at least they had good homes to go to; neighbouring landholdings had snapped them up. Other than the airships, there was nothing in the sky. He basked for a moment in the wondrous heat of a rare sunny day in Glasgow. The sun seemed brighter and the sky more blue. He might actually miss the place.

Under his feet he felt the generators increase their output. He laughed, startling a South Street docker. But they had to be careful. The European Block reacted badly, and with force, to the slightest rumour of an unauthorised flight. The Block's power over local matters had increased and their control of the Spindizzy technology was unchallenged. Only cities favoured by the elite were given flight status. Lisbon, whose star was in the ascendant, was on the east coast keeping a watchful eye over the Battle for Falkirk; its presence overhead ensured that both sides kept within the rules of engagement.

The Whiteinch airfield nestled between the bank of the River Clyde and South Street. It was empty now. The last of the airships had cleared their pylons. The few ships that were going to be travelling with them were securely tethered down.

Kim appeared from nowhere and leaned in close to his ear. 'That's a sight that never gets tired,' she said.

'You startled me,' he said, turning to catch her smile. She tilted her head back, regarding him.

'Sorry about that. I'm too excited.' She reached up to tease the fringe away from his eyes.

'How is everyone?' he asked.

'Better than I could have hoped. Doctor Gibbs has a handful of them in residence; they're getting their injections from the last of the hospital stock.

'I heard rumour of a still in operation,' he said.

'Really? I heard rumour about who set it up.'

'I couldn't possibly comment on that,' James replied, looking down at his feet with a distinctly mischievous look in his eyes. 'And the other residents?'

'They're at the Centre: all safe and accounted for.'

'And all stations are manned?' he asked.

'They should be. Come on, we need to get ready ourselves. MacKenzie will be expecting us.'

He nodded. They crossed the deserted street and hurried through the technicians' accommodation in Ferryden Court to the North Portal tunnel building where the Spindizzy Control Centre was housed. In the control room the technicians were checking every detail of the Spindizzy's operation. The perimeter nodes of the force field would keep the landmass in one piece. The turbine that once fed the Clyde Tunnel was now serving to cool the vast underground engineering system. The whole exercise was a miracle, especially since the City Chambers hadn't caught wind of it. Certainly they suspected; they had their spies, but the people of Whiteinch had done the best they could, just like those in Fort William and Crianlarich. The limited freedoms awarded them as a landholding had been exploited to the full. The time of their ascension was at hand.

James brought himself out of his daydream. He must be focused, alert.

'System status?' he demanded.

The tone betrayed his tension. MacKenzie, the settlement's engineering chief, wouldn't accept a disrespectful instruction from anyone. Given a safe and successful launch, she'd have revenge for that but James didn't mind. She'd put in a lot of work to make this day a success.

'We've run exhaustive tests on the drive and the nodes,' she said checking the scrolling readout on the monitor at her desk, 'and the generator is burning nice and hot. It won't run for long though.'

'The generator isn't up to it?' asked Kim. She had her own business to take care of back at the Centre but she loved the Portal Tower.

'I didn't say that,' said Mackenzie, looking up and giving her a quick smile. 'The generator is sound but whether we have the juice it needs is another story. We have enough for launch and to get to the rendezvous point but after that I just don't have the maths.

'And the rest?' asked James, looking over a table covered with reports. 'The drive and the nodes...?'

'They'll be fine. We've had some attempts at sabotage.' She shook her head at his look of surprise. 'But they weren't serious until today. I've got the Bowrie stationed on the wall to supplement security.'

'Seriously? The local gang?'

'Yeah,' MacKenzie said. 'In scuba gear doing runs on the dockside. I pity the fools who try and make their way in uninvited.'

'I'm impressed!' he called, over the suddenly rising drone of the turbine.

'That's the drive entering the final phase before launch,' she shouted, over the roar of the machines, catching his question from his raised eyebrow. 'It'll quieten in a minute.'

He turned his attention to the security monitors while MacKenzie studied her reports. He was worried about perimeter security despite the enthusiastic lads of the Bowrie. Moving through the cameras he could see Henrietta Street empty between the wilderness of Victoria Park and the transient camp just outside the Thornwood gate.

'Hey, guys! Its empty!' he yelled, pointing at the image of the Thornwood gate and the camp. Where is everyone?'

'Hells,' muttered Kim.

'I need to check it out. It might be nothing.' He turned to Kim. 'Get back to the Centre. There's less than thirty minutes until launch.'

He started towards the door but Kim caught his arm and moved in close.

'Be careful,' she said softly.

'I'll be back soon,' he said, and kissed her.

James stood in the badlands of Partick. It was a place decent people feared. The thirty-foot gate was behind him and a few of the Bowrie's most reliable boys were keeping lookout. Lisbon was on its way. He'd got the call before entering no man's land. He looked around the tenement ruins of Thornwood, the burnt out towers of the old Glasgow Harbour.

'You can come out now, Dougal,' he called. His voice rang clear through the silent wasteland. 'I know you're there.'

There was a moment of silence before he heard footsteps. Then, flanked by a pair of officers, out stepped the Lord Provost of Glasgow.

'The Provost?' came Kim's voice through his earpiece.

'Who else?' he answered. 'Bring the launch forward. Do it now. We've been found out. Lisbon will be on us soon.'

'But you're past the limits! You'll be left behind!'

Dougal, the Provost, stepped forward with his retinue in tow. Mackenzie's heart sank as she saw the colour drain from Kim's face.

'He's right,' she said. 'We have a visual on Lisbon. They'll be on top of us in minutes. We have to launch now!'

'Hold on!' Kim shouted. 'Where are the node controls?'

The Provost prodded a finger sharply in James' chest. 'I'll enjoy this,' he said. 'You've always been a thorn in my side, James. We know what you're up to. It's too late. No one leaves. Not you, not anybody.'

The officers lifted their guns. James stepped back raising both hands.

'Hey, we can talk about this.'

'Oh, it's too late for talk now, James,' said the Provost, his grin widening. 'You shouldn't have used your influence on the council to try and help your friends to escape. You should have known it would get back to me.'

Over Dougal's shoulder James could see the city mass of Lisbon in the distance.

'Back up to the gate, James,' said Kim's voice in his earpiece.

The officers advanced, prepared to fire.

'Launch now, for gods sake, Kim!'

'Back up to the gate, James. Just do it.'

He stepped slowly backwards. The Provost watched his retreat with relish. James felt a subtle change in pressure in front of him as his back touched the gate. Then they fired. He saw the muzzle of the three rifles flash and heard the three shots fire in quick succession.

Then nothing.

He opened his eyes to see the Provost's confusion and rage. Then he understood. Laughing and crying with relief he reached his hand out to touch the invisible wall of the force field and he heard Kim in his ear laughing with him. He was still laughing as the ground before him fell away and the heavens raced to meet him. Climbing slowly at first, the landholding of Whiteinch raced to the heavens, picking up speed with every second. They would soon join Fort William, Crianlarich and the others.

Whiteinch was no longer tethered.

Whiteinch was free.

Whiteinch was in flight.

WHITEINCH CROSS
Megan Wylie (age 10)

Hear the cars
Trees swishing
Feel the cold
Smell the paint
Our friends
On the wall
Thumbs up
Blue skies
Cool.

THE BUFFALOES
William McIntyre

The Royal Antediluvian Order of Buffaloes is a non-religious, non-political men's organisation whose main aim is to assist local charities. The Buffaloes have been active in Glasgow since 1902 when the first Glasgow lodge opened. The Caledonia Institute, where Glasgow lodges meet up and gather for social functions was originally in the Gorbals, but moved to Dumbarton Road, in Whiteinch, in 2006. The Caledonia Institute has raised close to £100,000 over the last 20 years, with last year's appeal raising £11,223 for Diabetes Scotland.

The Buffaloes began in the 1720's as The Lushington's, a group of theatre workers in London who met in the Lushington Bar. They travelled round the country with their shows and put on public performances in the town squares; after their impromptu performances they passed round a hat and donated all the money they collected to the poor. These performances were usually clownish and they earned the new name ' The Buffoons.' The idea spread round the country and many different branches were formed.

In the mid 1800s the organisation was renamed The Buffaloes. The name was picked because of stories of American Indians using the buffalo to provide food, clothing, tents and even tools to hunt; the name was to symbolise great strength providing for the family without waste. Perhaps understandably, the name was not popular in the United States: the American branch voted to call themselves the Elks.

The most famous members of The Buffaloes were Fred Flintstone and Barney Rubble; the Stone Age cartoon characters went to Buffalo meetings every week. The production company Hanna- Barbera wanted them to be members of a men's organisation. After much research they decided that the Buffaloes was the one group that could not cause offence due to their non-religious, non-political ideals.

FROM THE ROAB HANDBOOK

The Royal Antediluvian Order of Buffaloes is a social and benevolent fraternal organisation open to anyone over the age of 18, who is a 'true and loyal supporter of the British Crown and Constitution.' Its aim is to aid members in need and their families, and the families of deceased members as well as to support other charitable groups.

Justice, Truth, Philanthropy.
Nemo Mortalium Omnibus Horis Sapit.
No Man Is At All Hours Wise.

THE NEWSAGENTS
Allan Kennedy

When I was a baby, my family moved into a ground floor flat with a garden in Whiteinch overlooking Victoria Park. Ten years later we moved to a mid-terraced villa, still overlooking the Park, and I lived there till I was in my twenties, when I left for good. I never returned, but you can't live in Glasgow without at least passing through Whiteinch, thanks to the tunnel. We think of the past as being behind us, but sometimes it can sneak up and tap you on the shoulder. When I started looking into my family tree (what do you mean, mid-life crisis?), Whiteinch had simply been where I lived; I hadn't really seen Whiteinch at all.

For me, it was a place to play, go to school and ultimately leave. The world of adults was remote, uninteresting and utterly inexplicable to me. For me, like all the children I knew, the Park was the centre of the universe. It was full of possibilities for fun and adventure: playing football, usually twenty or more a-side, fishing for sticklebacks in the pond, or sailing a toy yacht if you were lucky enough to have one. I even ended up in the pond three times. Once, I was thrown in by the big boys, but even as a child it was only knee deep. Another adventure was cycling round the old boathouse to build up speed, cycling downhill towards the pond and then whizzing off round it. I missed the turn once, and cycled straight into the pond. The final time I fell in was when I was showing off, wearing my new cowboy outfit and walking on the handrail of the bridge. I slipped, and a sad and sorry cowboy squelched home. Being chased by the parkies was always good, scary fun. The building of the Tunnel and Clydeside Expressway eventually removed large chunks of the park, but my horizons had expanded by then and it had little impact on my life.

My Dad had a newsagents shop in Whiteinch. Once there had been two shops, known locally as Big Downie's and Little Downie's. My aunt eventually married the son of the owner and emigrated to New Zealand. Her husband flew with bomber command during the war. He was shot down over the channel, and spent many hours in the water before being rescued. He never recovered from his experiences, and although he had a successful business in New Zealand, he took his own life.

During the depression, the back shop was turned into an informal social club for the local men. They gathered to read the papers and play cards, to smoke or just while away the time. This was the community in action; Red Clydeside was as much about mutual support through hard times, as it was about industrial action. The news that war was brewing turned out to be good news for many. Suddenly there was a massive increase in demand for ships, so jobs were plentiful and money started coming into the houses. My eldest cousin, now 86, remembers suddenly being spoiled with pocket money. The elation about work being available soon paled as the war started, and news of the dead and injured filtered home.

Hard times were not in short supply. I remember being asked at primary to go to the door of a girl who hadn't been at school for some time and ask after her. I went up a close to her door and she answered it herself, seemingly alone in the house. She was incredibly pale, but my overpowering memory is of the inside of the flat seeming to be in black and white; it was dark, dirty and shocked me considerably, even then.

The shops eventually changed hands, and after the war my father took one as a newsagent, now Kennedy's, where he worked until he retired. It wasn't the only shop, of course. There was Galbraiths, the Aberdeen Fish Shop, two butchers, Nicol's Stores, and many others. There were two café's: Macari's and Pacitti's (both of Italian origin of course), and a chip shop. My father represented a change to the family tradition; his four brothers had all worked in Barclay Curle's shipyard. In my family tree, Occupation: Journeyman Riveter is a recurring theme. In more recent years the Kelvingrove Museum held an exhibition of shipbuilding, where you could handle the equipment the workers used. I tried to pick up a riveter's hammer and couldn't believe how heavy it was! I could never have done that for a living.

My grandmother didn't want a career in the shipyards for the baby of the family, feeling that he wasn't cut out for it. Instead, my father worked in a grocer initially, got married, and then was conscripted. He served with the Royal Artillery on coastal defences in England, and then was shipped to India for the onslaught on Japan. The bombing of Hiroshima and Nagasaki happened while they were in transit. Japan surrendered, so he never saw action. When he returned, he took on the newsagent's and became an integral part of Whiteinch. Mum worked in a munitions factory during the war, operating a mill lathe, but returned to being a housewife afterwards. My parents took in a family friend on his return from the war. The friend had been a POW in Japan, and returned to find his young brother now acting as head of the house and resenting his return. The difficulties were eased by his moving in with my parents till things settled. Such family conflicts weren't uncommon after the war, but are little recorded.

The shipyards employed thousands; I remember seeing them pouring out through the gates when work finished and being quite frightened by the sheer volume of people rushing to get out. It reminded me of the cattle stampedes shown in cowboy movies. Several times we got tickets to see launches, and the memory of the clouds of rust swirling as the drag chains took the strain remains vivid even now. My sister married a shipyard worker, and soon emigrated to America. Many other relatives also emigrated. They travelled to Hong Kong, Canada, America and one became a missionary in India. Some came back for the occasional holiday but none ever returned to live in Scotland.

The shop survived largely on selling newspapers and cigarettes to workers going to and from the shipyards. It opened at 6am and closed at 6pm, with the busiest periods immediately before the yards opened and closed. There was a major exception to this one day, when virtually all the men were late for work. The 'last tram' had run on the previous day, and its noise had acted as a communal alarm clock for years. When it didn't run, they all slept in.

I never knew my Grandparents; they died before I was born, but I heard the stories of how my great great uncle would walk from his home, 'Viewfield' in Balshagray to North Street to play cards with my grandfather. His name was John McLean and he became a local celebrity. He worked his way up through Barclay and Curle shipyards to become a director of the company and was knighted to become Sir John McLean. He was a prominent mason, a huge organisation at the time, and became Patron of Partick Thistle Football Club, whose first home was in Whiteinch. He was given the honour of formally opening Victoria Park. His name is still on the gates at Victoria Park Drive North. I have looked for his house, but I suspect it was demolished to make way for the tunnel approaches.

Whiteinch was a 'dry' area. This was unusual in Glasgow and owed much to the influence of the International Order of Good Templars, a temperance organisation which met locally and was dedicated to the abolition of alcohol. Temperance hotels had existed in Scotland and elsewhere, but were on the brink of extinction as I was growing up. The I.O.G.T. had been big in Scotland, but was never big enough to really challenge the west of Scotland's drinking culture. By the time I was growing up, the members were ageing and new recruits were few and far between. The Orange Lodge met in other rooms within the same halls as the I.O.G.T., but took a different stance on alcohol. Although a dry area, there was a Social Club which served alcohol to members. It was positioned directly opposite Jordanvale Church of Scotland, and it was joked that it catered for those who 'hunger and thirst after righteousness'.

As shipbuilding died, the Clyde clogged with silt. Few ships are built anywhere on the Clyde now; the work they brought has disappeared and not been replaced. The shop was demolished, along with all the others in that stretch of Dumbarton Road, and the tenements above them. New homes stand on the site now; better houses, often far more attractive than what went before, but it is no longer a place I recognise. When I walk along Dumbarton Road and through the park, I never see a face I recognise from the past. Perhaps my contemporaries have all gone, or perhaps I simply fail to recognise them.

THE CLYDEBANK BLITZ
Joyce Ito

In Whiteinch, Glasgow, on 30th January 1933, Mary entered the world kicking and screaming. There was no midwife to be found and her father gently rinsed the blood away. At the same moment a man called Adolf stood to attention as he was sworn in as the German chancellor. The crowds formed outside, elated, to celebrate his election. Mary's father listened to the radio while he watched his new daughter sleep.

Her earliest memory was her father shining his new boots to a high gloss and her mother crying terrified, hidden tears into his bag packed for the long journey. The next time Mary saw his boots they were scuffed and thin. The doctor had sent for him on compassionate leave when they thought that she might die. Mary was afraid when she saw him. He looked so pale and gaunt that she thought he came from one of her fever dreams. As her eyes focused on her father's altered face, Adolf pored over a blueprint of airtight chambers.

Mary missed her father. He used to read her stories, and she'd memorise bits from the book to read back to him. She was looking forward to being able to read properly, but after the bomb landed on her school she stopped learning. The bomb didn't explode, but Mary's mum was so bad with her nerves they had to leave Possilpark to live in Whiteinch with her grandparents. Mary felt as if the Germans had scooped up her school and her friends as well as her father and flown away with them in one of the planes.

Mary's grandparents owned a small confection and tobacco shop in Whiteinch and they lived in a room behind the shop. They had an Airedale terrier called Daisy and Mary would take Daisy for walks and tell her all about school in Possilpark, Miss MacDonald, her teacher, and Josephine, her best friend. She thought Josie would probably have another best friend now. Sometimes she would talk about her dad coming home when they had won the war. She wondered what would happen if they didn't win, but was careful not to say that out loud.

In Germany Adolf's friend Martin gave him a present of a beautiful German Shepherd dog. He named the dog Blondi. Adolf's girlfriend, Eva, was jealous of the dog and kicked him under the dinner table.

Whiteinch was near the docks where the ships were built and was much more dangerous than Possilpark in the north of the city, but Mary's mum felt safer and didn't cry so much. Mary got letters from her father but she couldn't read them and didn't like to keep asking her mum. She kept them folded in her storybook even though she was too big for the stories now. She was afraid of losing them, and afraid her father would be disappointed that she hadn't learned to read when he got back.

On the 13th March 1941 Adolf and Martin gave the order for the Luftwaffe to bomb Clydebank. The first bomb landed on the Yoker distillery two miles from where Mary and Daisy crouched in the narrow corridor at the back of the shop. The bombs landed all night and, though none landed in Whiteinch, the blast broke all the windows. Daisy peed the floor.

The next day Mary's mother wouldn't get out her bed. Granda grabbed Mary's hand and dragged her outside.

'The wean's got more gumption than you, Maggie,' he said.

There was broken glass everywhere, and looters had stolen everything from the shop. Granda was awful angry. They walked Daisy and Granda kept talking to himself.

'If it's not enough we're getting from the bloody Germans without this: and Maggie whinin' in her bed like a five year old. It's just as well the wean's got a level heid on her: and ma boy out there in uniform.'

He rattled on. Mary tried to memorise what he was saying, for thinking about later. She listened to the adults a lot now, but she was used to only understanding bits, keeping some for later, saving questions for the right time and place and person so that they didn't know what she was really asking.

Mary and her Granda wandered through the streets. Sometimes they stopped to talk to the neighbours, though Granda seemed to want the quiet. Then Daisy wagged her tail at a strange man and the man kicked her: just kicked her right on the nose, for nothing at all. Granda punched the man and they were punching and kicking and Mary could see the man was crying but she didn't know how to tell her Granda that he should stop and then they did stop and the man was crying on the kerbside and saying he was going to the morgue to look for his wife and then Granda was crying as well.

That day Mary's cousins from Clydebank arrived. They were all right but their house was wrecked. Mary's big cousin, Jim, still had the toilet door handle from his house in his hand when he arrived. It was white with a blue flower on it. Mary asked him what it was and he stared at it for ages and then laughed and laughed and there were big tears running into his beard. Mary's mum didn't want to let them stay; she said there wasn't room. Granda said he'd put her out in the street if it wasny for the wean and the Clydebank cousins could stay as long as they liked.

In April 1945 Adolf poisoned Blondi to ensure his cyanide tablets were effective. A few days later he and Eva committed suicide. The war ended on May 8th 1945 but Mary's father was in Poland and didn't return till October. He said Poland was the worst. He barely spoke, but settled in an armchair rolling tobacco into little white tubes and drinking whisky from a silver hip flask. He slept at odd times of the day and paced through the night. He didn't care that Mary hadn't learned to read.

THE BOWLING GREEN
Kyle Kaney (age 10)

I was walking down the street to buy a doughnut with Josh when we noticed the gate to the Bowling Green was unlocked. The padlock was gone and we saw that the gate looked new.

Josh asked me, 'Have you ever seen inside?'

I shook my head.

Josh pushed the gate and it swung open. We stepped in. There was a big square of grass and at the other end stood a girl dressed in a pinafore. I knew her from somewhere then I remembered her from a photo on the wall at home.

'Weird,' I said to Josh. 'That looks like my Ma when she was wee.'

'Look,' said Josh. 'It's only just been built. The walls are new, and the grass is only just laid.'

'Stephen!' shouted the girl. 'Come and play!'

I was about to shout back, 'I'm not Stephen!' when we saw a wee boy wearing long shorts run past us and towards my Ma.

I put my hand up and waved but my ma looked right through me. Josh reached for my arm.

'Let's get out of here,' he said, 'in case we get stuck.'

When we stepped back through the doorway, the street was just the same as before. Josh grinned at me.

'There's still a queue for the doughnuts,' he said.

2: Tenements

SHORTS
Carl MacDougall

I'd never heard of Whiteinch till Eric Gilmour took me home to meet his sister.

When I think of them in their kitchen with the sticky floor and the father who shouted at Myra and hit Eric across the back of the head, there's a doubled memory, a memory of an actual incident, but it comes with another memory, a false memory that has been with me all my life, that describes and defines me, an attempt to remember something that can not be found.

My father went to work and never came back, walked out the door and vanished. He lifted the hair at the back of my neck, picked up his haversack and left.

Twelve hours later we learned he'd been killed, run over by a train and identified only by his ring that said Love Marie and the date of their wedding inside the band.

I didn't find out till the funeral was over, when my mother collapsed into another fit of wailing and I went into the bedroom where she and her sister were sitting on the bed: My Daddy's dead isn't he? I said.

And my mother said, Go out and play.

I thought he'd gone to Oban because he didn't want to be with me and it was a great relief to know he was dead. And that made me feel guilty.

As I got older, I knew I carried a missing memory. We all have memories we did not experience. Memories of incidents that actually happened mingle with the common memories we find in newspapers, radio and television programmes. Family memories lie between them, no man's land, enhancing and cluttering both.

The memories I have of my father are mainly family memories. Through them I met someone I scarcely knew and he has become part of me. Family memory tells me my father was loveable, witty, handsome, smart, a lovely dancer and a good singer with a lively sense of mischief, a man who fought personal and family battles, a hero. And that is how I remember him, how he was given to me.

Like many children, I fantasised about having different parents. The thought that I might have been a foundling developed into an obsession with my past and became a quest to discover who I was and who I might have been. I reconstructed events that happened and didn't happen, events that might have happened or almost happened. And when I started writing, I took on this journey, rewriting the past, pursuing an obsession with secret histories and untold stories, writing about things that happened, or as they might have happened, inventing people, imagining things being different and working from there.

All of this was fully developed and active by the time I was sixteen.

And the invented me, the things that could have happened, the people I knew but never met, was more important and far more real than dreary authenticity.

I met Eric Gilmour at the YMCA in Sauchiehall Street. Every time I went to the Lyric Theatre he was there.

I'd been told they had an interesting amateur drama group and was attracted by the idea of pretending someone else was me. I failed the audition. I simply wanted attention, for people to recognise me or acknowledge I was there. And I fancied the applause.

A week or two later, I met him at a tram stop. The day was grey and had been threatening rain. People were rushing home, expecting the city to turn on them, for the weather to become hostile and the streets to give them no protection.

He stepped out as a tram approached. You should come down and play table tennis, he said.

I did for a while. Boys in nicely pressed shorts and polo shirts wore plimsoles, used Slazenger bats and five star Dunlop Excel balls in the room downstairs. Upstairs there was bare bulbs and three tables on wooden trestles. The bats and balls were kept in a box and if you wanted to play you asked Eric at the counter that sold lemonade and Buttermilk Dainties.

I lost myself, changed in the way sport varies your experience and energises your participation, gives simple victories a status and forces you to confront disappointment with no one else to blame. Within a month I was playing downstairs and training for the team.

Alec Naylor was the coach. He hugged you when you won and gave me a bat he said no one wanted. You'll need to get a pair of shorts, he said. I played in the sandshoes I always wore.

Alec told me you need shorts, Eric said. I've a pair that would fit you. I'll get Myra to stitch them up for you. They're a bit wide, but she'll sort them.

Eric had flat feet and a stoop. I imagined the ex-Army shorts you sometimes saw on summer beaches revealing legs as white as bone.

Myra wants to know your leg measurement, he said. And do you want the shorts to come to mid thigh or above the knee? She says she'll maybe need to measure you.

Autumn. Evenings turned dark; we had the first fall of snow and green flecked apples.

You'll need to get your shorts, Alec said. We're playing at the High School next week. You'll need to look smart.

I told Eric. We took the tramcar along Dumbarton Road. I'd never been this far west and watched the city slide around me. Eric talked all the way and shook his head when the kind of wee man you never see now, bowly legs and a bunnet, took two stops to get up the stairs, lit a cigarette and started singing, Somewhere over the Rangers.

I don't know how people can let themselves go like that, he said walking down Scotstoun Street. It's a disgrace. People like that should be shot.

In the close, someone was cooking cabbage. The stair was dark and there was no lock on his door. We went into the kitchen. Myra was standing at the sink, their father was sitting in a chair by the fire.

This is Carl, Eric said.

That's a lassie's name, his father said.

It was a room where no one seemed to settle. Even the light from the street seemed unsure of its function, bright turning dark with sudden brightness. A dying bluebottle thudded into the glass. Myra put the dishes away. The father riddled the embers in the grate, shook his paper and crossed his legs. Eric and I stood in the room.

Myra took a tape from the drawer. Let's get you measured, she said.

The father hit Eric on the back of the head. Idiot, he said. You told me you wouldnae be back till eight.

It was ten past seven.

I looked at the wall while Myra knelt in front of me. She hummed while she put the tape round my waist and held it at the front with her left hand while she moved it across my stomach.

That's not too tight, is it?

Eric moved to the window and looked out across the backs. Myra wrote the measurement onto a pad of pale blue Basildon Bond writing paper.

That's for letters, her father said. Don't waste it.

Myra looked up at me, smiled and shook her head. Then she pressed the back of her hand against my cock. I think mid-thigh's nice, she said.

I was sure I was going to come. She took the other measurements quickly and stood.

All done, she said.

Right, the father said. You can beat it.

Eric nodded and we stood at the door. If you asked Myra she'd go out with you, he said. She likes you. Wait here.

I heard the old man raise his voice. Myra had her coat on.

We could go to the Tivoli in Crow Road, she said. I don't know what's on, but it's a better class of cinema, a bit nearer the West End.

I've no money. We could go to the pictures another night.

The father was shouting and I heard a thump.

It's raining, she said. We could just stay here.

We moved down to the landing. She opened her coat.

Do you know what to do? she said.

Yeah.

Have you come already?

No.

I thought you came upstairs.

Nearly.

That was a laugh, eh.

I tried to count to fifty, do the eight times table and think of walking through the Laraig Ghru. It was hopeless.

I'll give Eric your shorts, she said.

I got soaked dodging into closes along Dumbarton Road, so I ran till I exhausted myself and stood beneath the railway bridge, breathless, leaning into the stone that smelled of dust, trying to evade the cloud of darkness that had swept across my father.

1245 DUMBARTON ROAD
Kenny Macdonald

My mother and father bought their first house from the factor in 1959. The house, which cost £500, was a room and kitchen at 1245 Dumbarton Road. Not long after this, my brother was born; I came along eighteen months later. We were on the second floor in the middle house. No-one called this kind of house a flat, as they do now. My brother and I slept and played in the room and our mum and dad slept in 'the kitchen': the room we ate, bathed and sat in during the day and evening. The settee doubled as a bed at night. Of course we had no bathroom but we had an outside toilet, used only by us, adjacent to Mrs Baxter's door on the landing. My mother said she would never have taken a house where we had to share a toilet with anyone else.

Next door lived Mrs Baxter. She was a small, round woman. I don't remember her face but she would talk to my mum on the stairs and my mum seemed to like her. The thing I did remember was her cough. You would hear her coughing through the wall or when you were out on the landing. It was the worst cough I had ever heard. For years, when I heard the name Baxter, I remembered only the sound of her coughing rather than her face. Baxter was the sound she made when she was in full flow.

On the other side was Mr Young. I don't remember a Mrs Young but I think there was one and I don't remember them having children but I think they did; maybe they were older than us. My grandfather was also Mr Young and years later, when he moved to the high flats in Blairdardie, our old neighbour Mr Young became his neighbour.

Upstairs was a family called Smith. My mother didn't like them. She talked about them having parties. I don't remember hearing any parties, let alone getting an invitation. There were a boy and girl in the house, Jimmy and Linda. They seemed nice and we played together once or twice. Also upstairs there was a family called McRae. My mother didn't like them either. The boy was called Paul and there was a girl. I don't know her name but I remember the morning she was killed by a car on Dumbarton Road. I didn't understand about death but I knew it was not a good thing. The family moved away not long after.

Mrs Vaughan lived downstairs. She ran one of the local shops, maybe the newsagent. She had a dog, a large, hairy German Shepherd. It was a lovely dog; all the kids would call its name, Yogi. One night, Mrs Vaughan's house went on fire. My brother was at the Boys Brigade. In her panic, my mother forgot this until I reminded her, and searched every corner of the house looking for him so we could get out. My dad wasn't at home either, he was working. We got out with the help of other neighbours and a wet towel wrapped round my head, to stop me choking. I can still smell the smoke. The fire was really bad. I saw the charred body of the cat lying out in the backcourt the next day. Neither Mrs Vaughan nor Yogi was home at the time. When my brother came home from the BB, he saw the fire engines outside and thought we were all dead.

One of the people who helped us that night was Mrs Dunn, who lived with her husband Sam across the landing from Mrs Vaughan. No matter the weather or occasion, Mrs Dunn always wore white gloves. She was an older woman with a grown up daughter Dorothy. My mum said she was a bit of a bum, always talking about how well her daughter was doing. She helped my mum sometimes, probably knowing that she was not always doing as well as her daughter. Mrs Dunn had a twin sister who also wore white gloves. You couldn't tell them apart.

Outside of the close was another world. Silvio's chip shop was a short walk away. As a huge treat my brother and I would get sixpence worth of chips some Saturday nights. Silvio was Italian, a really friendly man, always with a big smile and a silver Volvo car. We didn't know anyone else with a car. My mother said he looked like an Italian film star. At that time there was an Odeon cinema at the end of the building. On Saturday mornings, my brother and I went with all the other kids to the matinee. We thought it was amazing to have a cinema next door to where we lived. Sometimes a pop group played on the stage during the interval. I wonder if they became famous?

Just before you got to the cinema there was a café called the Commodore. When my dad worked in Connell's shipyard in Scotstoun, he would meet us at the café on his way home on a Friday night and buy us a wee paper bag full of white chocolate mice. He sometimes bought my mum a Fry's Chocolate Cream. My mum also took us to Connell's once to see a ship called The Vanguard being launched.

The other place, of course, was Victoria Park. Whiteinch Park, we called it. You could see it from our the window, up Elm Street, and we went every day, by ourselves, my brother making sure I got across the main road safely. My mother was a nervous wreck watching us from the window: I felt her watching us cross. The Fossil Grove was a great place for exploring, even without understanding its historical significance. In the Summer, we took paddle boats on the pond, the parky shouting not to take them under the wee bridges. We did it anyway. In Winter the pond was solid with ice.

Even the shops held a fascination for us. At night, my brother and I in our bunk beds, him on the top, me beneath, asked each other were we facing Galbraith's way or Templeton's in Scotstoun way, before we went to sleep. The fruit shop along Dumbarton Road just had floorboards and the woman was bent over like she had a sore back. The smell in the shop, which is in my nose to this day, was of beetroot boiling in the back. Mum bought some, wrapped in newspaper by the woman who wore gloves with the fingers cut off. She gave Mum wee extras for making soup because we didn't have much money. People helped each other then. Mum cut the beetroot and put it in a sandwich for us.

Things changed when my brother started school at Whiteinch Primary. Before that we had always had been so close, always together. Mum took me along at playtime with a playpiece for him; something like two digestive biscuits with butter in a paper bag, squeezed through the railings to him. He seemed happy but for me it was as though he was being contained there. Two years later, when I started there, I found I enjoyed it. There were a lot of nice kids, most of them new to me. There was a boy there called Rashid. He was the first Asian person I had met apart from the men that used to come round the doors selling housewares. He didn't speak good English and he seemed sad. I was fascinated by him because he was different. I worried about him.

BELINDA'S HIDEAWAY
LIME STREET
WHITEINCH
Ellen McMillan

Belinda ran a duster over the imposing double doors, before closing both
to prying eyes. She liked the black paintwork. The brass letterbox and
doorknob, she left untouched. The hallway was dark; this side of the house
had no windows. She climbed the wooden stairs to the musty attic, where
her baby was.

They, she and her father, had moved here in 1907 a year after the
property was built. The house was one of the Mackay cottages of Whiteinch.
Belinda was pregnant but not at this stage showing, which was just as well,
her father said, people wouldn't like it. If her father said so it must be right,
although Belinda didn't really understand why. Trust me, her father had said,
and Belinda had done just that. Belinda had seen babies but she just couldn't
understand where the one inside her came from. Her father said that God
had sent it. They had to move from their old house; Belinda's mum had
already left. She didn't know where her mum had gone. Her father said she
had left during the night and people would talk, so they'd had to find another
house. Lime Street was nice and as Belinda's tummy grew she spent all of her
time indoors. Father said it was for the best.

There was too much work for one person and Father had hired a
lady to clean the house. Her name was Nan. Belinda didn't like her. She had
to stay in her bedroom when the Nan the cleaning lady was there, or father
said there would be trouble. People talked, he said, and so Belinda remained
in her room but she didn't like it. Father said she should hide her tummy, but
it was very hard to always remember- and so he had put a girdle on her. She
could hardly breathe, but father said that was the only way. It was easier just
to sit with the girdle on and so Belinda sat most of the day. She started sewing
to keep her occupied; she made a little blanket for the baby that father said
would come. They had tried to teach Belinda hard things at the school where
they used to live. The teacher told her father that Belinda needed a special

school, that she was in fact, unteachable. Belinda stopped going to school; father said it was for the best. She cried at night while Father slept, she hadn't known why. She told her father she felt sad. Father said she made him angry.

Belinda had pains in her tummy for a long time before Father gave her the whisky. It tasted rotten. Father said he'd looked for the baby but God had taken it while they'd slept. Belinda couldn't remember anything. But there was a baby; Belinda found it in the attic in a shoebox. She put the little blanket she had made over it. It wasn't a pretty baby. She didn't tell her father, she didn't want to make him angry.

Father was happy for a time, then in 1964, he died and Belinda was left alone. Nan looked out for her and helped her shop and clean. Belinda liked Nan now. Nan baked her birthday cakes and took her for walks. Belinda had arthritis now; her hands and legs were sore. Nan told her to take it easy but she still liked to climb the stairs to the attic. There were bats in the attic. Nan complained of the smell. She said the bats smelled like a dead body.

Belinda lifted the shoebox out of the darkness and took the duster over it. Inside were some little bones and the blanket she had made all those years ago: she couldn't remember how many. It was long before father had died. She wasn't clever, Nan said. She cried a little, but not as much as she used to when she knelt over the box. She was old now; soon she would join her baby and her dearly beloved father. She still wore the girdle at night, to stop another baby growing while she slept.

TABLE AT THE WINDOW
Dorothy Morrison

In Back Street Pine we
hummed and hawed then chose it:
oval, drop-leaf, voluptuous pedestal
three feet. Grandma would have
approved the use of her legacy, being
cook and baker, preserve-maker, and
shy entertainer.

Bay window looking westward to
Yoker and east towards town, the
park, the gusset and shops. Ahead, a
terrace of houses, a vet's where
sombre faces came and went.
Poorly pets in cages. Three flights up, the
light from the sky transformed the
north-facing aspect. Endless traffic swish-swished on
wet roads below.

I sat and looked out on the
journeys of others. One or two could share the
view but when more came to visit, my
window on the world got only a cursory glance.
There were conversations to be had.

Tight fit of six people around our
table, full-out between two long walls:
pine unit on one; fyfestone feature on the other.
The trailing plant- 'Is that ivy tickling your neck?'
'I thought your wife's name was Jean?'
Laughter launched the nights.

Aspirations to elegance, Assembling
potential pairings; my first mouthful of tepid minted
pea soup. No microwave to zap each
bowlful. Polite silence as they pretended that all was
well as we supped. Funny how the evening never
warmed up either.

We ended with the pose (your idea, not mine). The
SOLD sign of the Estate Agent as you snapped my glee, waving
down to you one last time; and the man who turned to look as you
passed. You wiped your eyes, feeling bad; you sensed my
relief in deserting it all to go
many miles.

THE SHED
Natasha Gallacher (age 9)

Yesterday, Alisha came round to tell me she'd found something in the shed.
I grabbed my jacket and we slipped out the back way. It was getting dark and
the lane was deserted. We ran down muddy car tracks towards the shed and
stood outside, panting. Then I heard the scratching.

'That's him,' said Alisha. I could hear the blood in my ears.

We crept to the door and I wriggled the bolt slowly so as not to make
a single squeak. I opened it a crack and we both peered in. Inside, a giant
rat was cowering in the corner. He was white with evil, red eyes. He looked
at me a moment then he bolted for us. I banged the door shut and Alisha
jammed the bolt in place. He was going crazy in there, knocking over plant
pots and garden tools.

'D'you think we should tell? Alisha asked me.

I shook my head. 'No way. My Ma'll not let me out for weeks if
she knows.'

'What if he escapes?' said Alisha. We piled up a load of junk in front of
the door just in case.

Today Alisha came round for me on the way to school. When we turned the
corner into the lane, we saw the junk scattered all across the mud and the
shed door banging in the wind. Alisha grabbed my arm.

'Let's look for the tracks,' I said.

From the shed, the huge footprints led away down the lane in the
opposite direction.

'Alisha,' I whispered. 'He's gone towards the school.'

THE BOADY
Ellen McMillan

Janice appeared at my door. I could see her through the tulip glass panel.

'Hurry up,' she shouted. Her voice would have been more suited to a coalman than a twelve year old. She was months younger than me but much bolder in attitude.

'Where's the murder?' I asked, using one of my mother's expressions.

Janice pushed her head between the door opening.

'Doon the backroad, gaun toward Whiteinch. Hurry up,' she roared at me. 'Get yer coat, we're gaun tae see the boady.'

'What's happened?' I asked whispering, so my mother couldn't hear.

'Some guy got his heid chopped off and his boady's still there.'

I grabbed my coat. My mother's voice bellowed, 'And where are you off to madam?'

'Just out for a walk with Janice.'

'Don't you be long mind , lady, there's stuff to be done before your dad gets back.'

'Okay Mum.'

I ran for the door. Janice filled me in on the way. At the end of the square where we lived there were at least ten more kids all going to see the boady. Some guy had been killed on a piece of spare ground near the scrap yard we called Golfies. We went through all the possible suspects on the way, like detectives. Maybe it was a gang. It could have been his wife Naw a wife widnae chase him wi an axe. How do you know it wis an axe they used? Naebody knew. We speculated some more.

Finally we reached the spot where the victim should have been; there was only the outline of where he had lain. We were enraged; he had risen from the dead just to spite us.

'Hey, there's a bit of his heid.'

There was part of him still there: a little bit of hair covered scalp. We were relieved and kind of fascinated but it wasn't the same as a whole murder victim.

'Kinda looks like a wee mouse,' one of the bigger boys said. We nodded in agreement, but we were deflated. We hunted around the area, just in case the polis had moved him out the way, like some bizarre hide and seek: nothing. Eventually we made our way home along the back road. The journey seemed much longer returning. We all rehearsed our stories in case our parents found out were we had been, each warning the other to keep our mouths shut or we were all for it. Our parents were much more scary than the polis.

In the days that followed, we heard every theory regarding the death of the poor guy. It was a gangland attack; the scrappy owner had killed him for trespassing. We even heard that he had been chased all the way along the old railway track from Partick to Whiteinch before being killed. None of us ever really knew what had happened.

A few weeks later I was going to the Whiteinch Park with Janice. We never called it the Victoria Park. My mother looked over the top of her glasses and said, 'Don't go along the back road. There was a young man killed there.'

'I know,' I said without thinking.

'And how do you know that young lady?" my mother asked.

I gulped, grabbed my jacket and ran out the door saying, 'Janice told me.'

Sometimes not telling the whole story is a lifesaver.

3: People

SAMMY'S STORY
Samantha Mitchell

I was born in Partick then I moved with my Ma and sister to Drumchapel. We came back to Whiteinch when I was seven. I was an absolute horror when I was young. I put my mum through hell. I don't know why but I always felt I wasny good enough. I constantly had a chip on my shoulder. My Ma used to say, 'It's not so much a chip as a bag of totties.' My Mammy always praised me but everything would go wrong for me. See if we got walky talkies for Christmas, my sister's would work and mine wouldny. I had the bad luck. The only thing I did well was drawing. I always did that. It was the only thing I was good at.

I was a single parent for years. Then when the wee one started nursery, the nursery said to me, 'Why don't you go and do something?' As soon as they said 'College,' I thought, 'Aye.' So I went to Anniesland College at the Balshagray campus, to do an NC in Sculpture. By that time my Stepdad was ill with cancer. When I finished my NC I'd a show on and I wanted him to see it. I wanted them to see it, him and my Ma.

He walked it from Whiteinch to Thornwood to see my show, even though he had lung cancer. He was dead proud of me. That's when I realised what I was worth. They said, 'We've always been proud of you', but it was then I felt it myself. I carried on to do the HNC and the HND. For me to get a pass in anything, because I had to do the paperwork as well, it was something, you know. No matter how much you struggle you can do it. If I can do it, anyone can do it.

I don't think much about what the future holds for me. I want to do something for kids for the future. I'm going back to college to work voluntary with special needs students. I think now, when I help someone else, that's me paying off for being so terrible as a kid. The kids make art through their graffiti. I wish they could have something they could be proud of. See if kids get the chance to draw and paint, they're proud of it. Cos I think a lot have got chips on their shoulder same as me. I'd like to see adults getting involved with them more, not being scared to do stuff together. That's what I'd like to see.

JACKIE
Betty O'Hara

My family lived in Scotstoun: me, five sisters, one brother and our mum and dad. I remember as a little girl, waking up with the sun shining through the bedroom window. Great! My dad promised to take us all to the Whiteinch Park. I make my way to the bathroom for a quick wash, get dressed and into the kitchen where the porridge is bubbling away on the cooker and the plates are set out on the table. After porridge and buttered rolls we get all the things ready for the park. Dad gets his stuff for playing bowls on the green and we get our tennis racquets and the picnic basket with our jammy pieces and bottles of lemonade.

We walk along Danes Drive and enter the park at Westland Drive. The first place we make for is the fossil grove. The surrounding grounds are filled with lovely flowers and the colours and smells are so beautiful. It's strange and quiet and magical when we enter the grove. We stand and look down at all these trees that have been turned to stone. It's like an echo chamber and all our voices bounce off the walls and the ancient trees.

The lily pond outside the grove has real frogs and we can hear them croaking as we get near. We stand and watch them jumping about on the water, but we can hear the Salvation Army brass band playing and so we all run round and get seats round the bandstand. We spend an hour there listening to the music and munching away on jammy pieces and slices of clootie dumpling and drinking lemonade from tin cans. The band played all the tunes of the moment as well as hymns; Daisy, Daisy was my favourite and my Dad's was The Old Rugged Cross.

When the band finishes we run for the boating pond for a shot on the paddleboats. The boys have nets to catch fish in the pond. My big brother Jackie has a jelly jar full of baggie minnows. We have a last shot on the swings and its time to go home; mum will have the dinner ready. We're tired and happy and ready for our dinner as we go in the front door: joy of joy, the great smell of mince and tatties, our favourite. What a wonderful ending to a perfect day.

It's 1947 and I wake to the sound of the sirens. It's wartime and our brother Jackie is fighting with General Montgomery's desert rats. Each night we go through the same routine. In the hall we lay out our siren suits, one piece outfits that are easy to put on quickly in the dark, with our boots set out beside each suit. We put the leather Vanderbilt case with our birth certificates and other important papers beside the door. Then we go to bed and try to sleep until the sirens wake us up. We dive into our suits, lace up our boots, pick up the bag, the blankets and a flask and run for the Anderson shelter in our back garden. We sit packed like sardines and wait for the screech of the bombs. We are very lucky; most of the bombs have been dropped in Clydebank. Our windows are taped up to stop them breaking but they are still smashed from the blast. At least the taping has saved us from having broken glass everywhere.

Our windows are permanently blacked out and there are no street-lights. We have to be careful at night if we open the door to be sure we don't let out any light. Every close has a brick wall called a baffle wall at its entrance for protection from the bombs. People are always banging into the walls and doors in the dark, especially the men making their way home from the pub after a few pints.

I decide to do my bit for the war effort by joining the ambulance service. Now when the sirens go off I make my way to the ambulance depot at Kingsway and we go where we are needed. My First Aid knowledge is put to the test. Many people have lost their lives, some are taken to hospital, and many need First Aid. I'll not forget all those dead and injured people.

I had attended Victoria Drive Secondary School and we were all very proud when one of the first Victoria Crosses of the war went to John Hannah, one of our fellow pupils. His picture had pride of place in the assembly hall.

I had been training as a florist at Malcolm Campbell's in Byres Road, but I was told I had to leave to work towards the war effort. I was given a job as canteen assistant at Meechan's shipbuilding yard at Balmoral Street. I soon got used to the banging and hammering and the smells if oil and wood. The men were a jolly lot and always had a joke or a funny story to tell. There was one lad, Jimmy, who was fourteen. He was a cheeky boy, full of fun and always telling jokes. He really looked forward to a Friday because all the workmen gave him a wee tip for bringing their tea. Jimmy took the money straight to the second hand shop in Partick where he saving for a bike. I remember the day he finally got that bike. The brakes weren't all that good and it was a bit rusty, but Jimmy said he'd soon fix all that. He couldn't have been more proud if he'd just bought a Rolls Royce.

Everything was rationed; we had coupons for food and clothes Cigarettes were scarce, except for Pasha cigarettes which smelled foul. We often went to the Victoria picture house in Whiteinch. The program changed three times a week. If anyone lit up a Pasha all you could hear was 'put that out' they smelled so bad. After the pictures we went along the Dumbarton Road at Whiteinch. There was a close there on the ground floor that was a bakery. We could buy a roll for a halfpenny and then get a pennyworth of chips from the chip shop across the road to fill our rolls. Salt and vinegar, sheer heaven!

We met many different nationalities. The Americans who arrived thinking Scottish people went around in kilts and the only transport was carriages. The Americans introduced us to nylon stockings. They were so fine we washed them while on our legs, rubbed a towel over them to dry and kept them in a glass jar so they didn't snag. The nylons were kept for special occasions. There was a tattoo artist in Argyle St. we went to. He would paint on a heel and a seam right up your leg and we could choose a square, a diamond or a step heel. It stayed on for months and looked great with the leg tan we got from the chemist. We made our own face packs with Fullers earth and the white of an egg; the grey powder went sticky with the egg and stuck fast to your face so you couldn't smile or twitch a muscle. We had to decide whether to have our egg ration for breakfast or use it for a face pack.

My mother and aunt launched a frigate in Yarrows Shipbuilders. It was the first time a worker's wife had done this because of the great work the yard had done. Instead of the usual bottle of champagne they were given a small polished mallet with the ship's name and the date on it. They hit it so hard they put a big dent across it (the mallet, not the ship). The comment from Lord Yarrow was 'it's well seen it was a working man's wife that launched this ship.'

There were not many bombs dropped in Scotstoun or Whiteinch, though in Yarrows one of the shelters got a direct hit and the men from the night shift lost their lives.

There were so many sad times when our friends lost their loved ones. We lost our only brother Jackie. He was in the 7th Battalion of the Black Watch and survived the desert with General Montgomery and then survived Dunkirk. He was killed in Italy on the 1st of August 1943; he and three other men died when their dugout took a direct hit. He was only twenty-four. What a terrible waste of such a great man.

My son Jackie, named after his uncle, grew up to be a Royal Marine and now my grandson, Kevin, is in training for the SAS. I am so proud of them. I have promised myself one day I'll go and visit Jackie's grave in Sicily. It hasn't happened yet, but who knows, maybe one day.

MY DA
Cathie Caldwell

We stayed in a single end in Partick and we used to go to the park. My sister and I had to watch our two brothers. They would catch baggie minnows in a jam jar with string tied round the top to keep a hold of it. This day my brother Tommy fell in. It was bad because he had bronchitis. He was born in 1940; he used to take nightmares with the war. My mother would never take us to a shelter; she just kept us in the house. We got evacuated to Crossford in Ayrshire somewhere it was.

When we lived in Halkirk Street in Partick there was just a wee gas-light; the lamplighters used to go around. Then we got a room and kitchen in Castlebank Street. It had electric light. The front room window overlooked the Anchor Line ships. We used to look out and see the ships getting built. My father worked in Archibald Low and Sons, a brass moulders.

We'd a terrible time with my Da and the drink. We all slept together in the room, and my Da slept in the recess in the kitchen. Every Friday night, I can picture it now. He was the nicest man, but it was like Jekyll and Hyde. They called him Hobby because his name was Hobson. We could hear him coming all the way from the Best Bar on the corner of Halkirk Street and Merkland Street. Sometimes we used to hide under the bed. My mother used to go out and wash stairs, because we never had any money. He was just shouting and bawling, all the names under the sun. We had to put him to bed, me and my sister Martha, get him undressed and put him to bed. My mother never jailed him; she wouldn't.

I went to Dowanhill Commercial College to get shorthand and book-keeping and all that. My first job was at Thomas Black and Son, in Peel Street. I worked there for twelve years. My boss was nicer to me than my father, you know. I got on alright there. My boss, he'd a lot of property all over the place so he offered us a rented house in Kelvinhaugh Street. One day we just packed up and left my father. Left him in the bed.

I hated Kelvinhaugh Street where we lived in the bottom flat in the close. It had a bathroom; that was something. You'd rip up the newspaper in squares and put in on the string. We'd a bath and toilet, but no hot water. We went to Whiteinch Baths for a hot bath; it wasn't just for swimming.

I believe my father moved to lodgings in Maryhill. Anyway, he came back. I was fed-up with my mother crying. My Uncle Harry was found dead in his house around that time. When he retired he'd wanted to go and live with relations in Ireland but he never made it. All his money went to my Da and his sister. She stayed in Byron St. We met up with my Da; that was quite a thing, all this money in Uncle Harry's house. He wouldn't bank any of it.

My brother Tommy left first; he couldn't put up with any more, wouldn't have any more of it. And Martha and I were next. My boss again, he offered us this house in Medwyn Street, me and Martha. We didn't want to go but we had to. It was freedom. We managed. We papered and painted. Eventually we heard that my dad was in Stobhill Hospital. Martha and I used to go and visit him. It was cancer. I remember the time we went just at the end. He said he'd been out in the grounds. He was the loveliest man but he didn't remember birthdays. We got nothing. When he died, he left all he had to the relations in Ireland we'd never seen: left nothing for us. My Mum got something in the end. But it just shows you.

KATHY'S STORY
Kathy Clark

I was born in Whiteinch. The building I was born in was pulled down for
the Tunnel. It was a fantastic place. In the back court it was great. We used to
play houses and the boys would play as well. We got bricks and built a room
and kitchen. We used to play shops. We fenced them off and we had bits
of glass for money. The mothers all joined in; even the boys joined in. You
played the usual games: rounders or hide and seek. You all knew one another.
In those days women had their children in the house and you were taken
into a neighbour's house to sit. You wouldn't know what was going on right
enough: just, 'Sit there' until the child was born.

I was the oldest of four. We had a toilet inside so we were quite
fortunate. My dad worked in the Barclay Curle yard and then in John
Brown's. He drove the big crane. He used to take his cushion to work to sit
in the crane. Both my parents were Irish. My mum from Donegal and my
Dad from Omagh in County Armagh. We used to go every year to the farm
house. Mum packed a big trunk and sent it on ahead. We used to go on the
Cattle Boat from the Broomielaw, an overnight crossing. We'd go there for six
weeks' holidays every year.

I went to Saint Paul's primary in the building of the old Whiteinch
Neighbourhood Centre. The school was on the ground floor and the chapel
was upstairs. School was very strict and regimental. Secondary was more of
a problem with teachers throwing chalk and blackboard dusters at you. But
at Primary, see in the summer holidays, we still got our milk. We went round
to Whiteinch Primary and got our wee bottle of milk, every day. And it was
good milk: none of that semi-skimmed.

Whiteinch Ferry used to go from the street where Whiteinch Cross is
now: a pedestrian ferry across to Govan. We never paid, we just jumped on.
We'd play about in the swing park – it was the thrill of going on the ferry. It
was all grown-up. We didn't hang about in Govan: just went to the playpark
and came back again.

The backcourt had a washhouse. All the maws did a washing and took turns. They helped one another. People used to put on wee shows: the maws would get changed in the washhouse and then we'd put on a show in the backcourt and everyone would hang out their windows to watch. We'd all sing songs.

We were in Dumbarton Road, our backcourt was Medwyn Street. Mrs Adams lived opposite. On Saint Patrick's Day, Mum put up her green curtains and Mrs Adams put up her orange curtains, but it was a friendly battle.

The Rag and Bone man used to come round regular with his horse and cart. You gave him something – some clothing – and he gave you a balloon. We thought it was wonderful.

I went to the dancing in Clydebank every Sunday night. You went to chapel first then dancing afterwards. It was two shillings for the dancing and tuppence for the plate.

After I got married, we lived in Glasgow with our first child. In those days you spent your whole day washing and cleaning. You did everything by hand: it kept you busy! Then in 1964, my husband got a job in Singapore and we went to live there with the children. I was told, 'You'll get plenty of help with the children on the plane.' Did you what! Being in Singapore taught me that nobody's any better than me, and vice versa.

But things went wrong, and my husband left. It was a terrible stigma in those days, even if it wasn't your fault. I was devastated but you had to keep going for the sake of the baby. My daughter was eleven, David was ten when Barry was born. I stayed in Dundee on my own for a whole year. I went to Gingerbread there: that was a great help. It got that bad, I made a decision to come back to Glasgow, to be near my family. I've got a lot of faith; that's what got me through.

When Barry was three, I went back to work as a secretary at a solicitor's office, McClay, Murray and Spence. When you spoke to the boss it was all Mister and Missus. You didn't speak to the top lawyers when they spoke to you. After that, I got a job in social work as a secretary, typing all the reports. I remember one I typed where a chap had his children and his wife had left him. The social worker had written, 'I don't think this chap can cope with his children after all this,' and I said to myself, 'Wait a minute.' So I went to speak to the social worker. 'He's broken,' I said, 'He's in a terrible state but that doesn't mean he can't look after his kids.' So she changed the wording of the report so that he got to keep his children; I was so pleased. It made me very angry how they assumed there had to be two parents: it doesn't always take two; I don't think so anyway. They used to say, bad area, single parent I don't know if they still do that. I didn't change my standards because I was a single parent. If anything it makes you work harder to give your kids the best you can.

Now my children live near me, all in Glasgow. They're all married. See when my daughter was married, I gave her away. She said, 'You brought us up, Mum.' I was so proud. Now my oldest grandaughter is twenty and the youngest is two. The family look after me. The things they did for my birthday were unbelievable. They paid for my trip to Rome and then two meals out. I'm very lucky.

MARRIED AND 'SETTLED'
Marion Bernstein

Oh! I have sighed to read
The trials of this season;
Wife-murder seems, indeed,
An everyday transgression.

Too oft the marriage bond
Is one of fear and pain;
Affection true and fond
Should link that sacred chain.

Can home appear 'sweet home'
When 'husband' means a foe
And 'wife' a slave?–for some
Submit to have it so.

It seems to me such wives
Act rashly, at the least,
Like men who risk their lives
In taming a wild beast.

Beast-taming seems to be
Not quite a woman's mission;
The brutes might stay for me
In bachelor condition.

But, since you choose to wed
And risk your limbs and lives,
Consider what I've said
All ye unhappy wives.

Exert your common sense
And form a combination
For mutual defence
Against assassination.

HUMAN RIGHTS
Marion Bernsteim

Man holds so exquisitively tight
To everything he deems his right;
If woman wants a share, to fight
She has, and strive with all her might.

But we are nothing like so jealous
As any of you surly fellows;
Give us our rights and we'll not care
To cheat our brothers of their share.

Above such selfish man-like fright,
We'd give fair play, let come what might,
To he or she folk, black or white,
And haste the reign of Human Right.

Marion Bernstein made her living as a teacher of piano and music and the Post Office Directory listed her as living at 12 Craignethan Gardens, Partick, in 1900. She had published a book of poems Mirrens Musings in 1876, and her poems had regularly appeared in the 1870's in the Glasgow Weekly Mail. They were sometimes piously Christian in character, at other times of a radical feminism that speaks directly to the present age more than a century later.

The two poems printed here are taken from Mirren's Musings and appeared in the selection of eight poems by Marion Bernstein published in Radical Renfrew (ed. Tom Leonard) Polygon, 1990.

4: Centre

THE JANNY
Anon.

Tommy always works a Tuesday night. It's alright, as long as the young ones aren't acting up. They don't listen. When he tells them he won't put up with that kind of language, they laugh in his face. The lassies are the worst. They dance rings round him. He doesn't like asking them to leave because it makes him nervous about going for the bus later.

'There's one tonight,' says the girl from the church, 'we're not letting him in, he was causing trouble last week. Just in case he tries it on.'

'No bother, hen.'

'It's Jane', she says.

'Aye. Jane.'

He sits down behind the desk, with a cup of tea. Mary, she's a decent woman. She always sees he has a cup of tea. She should tell those kids to get out of her café, mind you. It's not his job to do that. He dunks his biscuit and opens the Evening Times. A group of youngsters pass the desk, heading for the Hall. It's not until they've passed that Tommy sees one of them is the lad that's barred.

'Hey, you!'

They all turn. Tommy points to the lad in the sports jacket. 'You've not to go in this week. That's what the lassie Jane said.'

'I'm not listening to you, old yin. What do you know about anything?'

The church girl is at the Hall door though, and she turns the boy away. He knocks over a chair on the way down the Hall and heads for the café. Tommy follows him through. Mary's a soft touch, she'll let him stay in there if he buys a can.

'Mary, this one's been thrown out of the Hall. Any problems, let me know and I'll put him out.'

'Who d'you think you are, ya bam? This centre's for all the community. That's young people as well. It belongs to us. You're just the janny.'

Tommy's neck is blotching red. 'You'd better take that cheek out your voice, son, he says. I'm not paid to take that'.

'This place is a lot of shite, anyway.' The lad's chair screams against the floor and he saunters off, hands in his pockets. He disappears into the toilets, banging the door.

'I feel sorry for them, Tommy', Mary says to him. 'They've nowhere to go and it's so cold out.'

Tommy shakes his head and takes up his place behind the desk again, finally getting a chance to read the day's news. He's almost finished his tea when the wee lad comes out of the toilets.

'I've left a present for you, pal. Just to say thanks.'

Tommy didn't know what the hell the boy was talking about. Some silly boy joke. It was Mary that says, 'Better go and check they toilets. I'd do it, but it's the men's and I'm not getting caught in there.' The stink hits him when he pulls the door. In the middle of the floor he's done it, the little bugger. What a nasty wee bastard he is. He holds his breath, but he still gags when he picks up the shit with a bit of toilet roll and flushes it down the toilet. Then he goes and gets the mop and bucket out of the cleaning cupboard and washes the floor.

When he's locking up, well after ten, he hears laughter coming from down the street. There he is, having a good laugh with his mates. Tommy has to walk past them to get to the bus stop.

'Aren't you going to say thank you for my present?' says the wee shite. Tommy keeps his mouth shut. He's got his eye on the strip of light at the main road, wondering how long till the next number nine comes.

RECOVERY
Robert McDermott

With elation you will greet yourself on arriving
As I have been there
Darkness cold and damp
Miserable years of days gone by
As I have recovered this broken body
It's time to make it start to heal
My mind is smashed by negativity
But nature sparks me into activity
The memories I have of traumatic past
Are replaced by hope.

THE FIGHTER
Robert McDermott

I was a young boy when I started boxing with the Dennistoun club. I went on to become Senior Scottish Champion. I fought for titles in the ABA finals in Manchester. I travelled the world fighting for Scotland - maybe a couple of hundred amateur fights. It was total dedication, I was going places. My maw used to fix all my gear for me, get it ready for the next day. On my nineteenth birthday I got the Ken Buchanan award. He was a world champion, a great fighter.

Then I started using drugs. I felt as if I'd already done most things in my life. That total dedication with the boxing, it messed my heid right up. It sickened me. I thought, This is far too much for me. The boys were drinking, taking drugs, seeing women. I thought, they're doing it, I'm gonny do it; it was an escape route.

It broke my maw's heart. She died not longer after that – it was me that found her. That's what made me be a real bad bastard. For twenty years I hated the world: addictions, jails, hospitals, loads of violence outside the ring. Prison was the only good thing because I did all these SVQs.

When I was twenty-four, I got offered money to come back. They didn't know I was still using. I'd work round it. Another five years' fighting I had, twenty-eight fights as a professional, at least ten world championships. I was a journeyman. It didn't bother me who I fought. All I thought was, how much? They sent me over to McGuigan's camp. I was sparring with him every day. I fought under the world champ bill, McGuigan v Eusebio Pedroza, in 1985 at Loftus Road. I've never been knocked out. I've fought some of our country's best, you know?

But I was into crime, getting jails, involved in street wars: heavy stuff. I never achieved total abstinence; I learned that later when I had to. It started with going home one day and the house was boarded up. My wife had bolted. She'd had enough. She always wanted to go back home to Liverpool. So I was running about the streets for a while. The Council hostels wouldny take me. I wouldn't do as I was told. I hated the system. That's why Hope House was my only option. It took me a couple of month of using on the Clydeside there, all black eyes, big lumps in my heid, thinking, This is end of the world stuff. I would've wiped the floor with them a couple of year ago – what's goin on?

I asked the other residents how long they'd been there and they were saying, fifteen year, ten year, seven year. I thought, No way! This is just another jail. So I saw the housing officer and asked him, How do I do it? He says, Best thing is do something wi yourself. I'd seen a poster for NA. I thought, they help addicts and there's nay bosses! I couldny believe it! I went to every group, all over: all different members. I thought, I'm really part of something that's a movement.

I was rough but I wasny strung out like I needed to run away and use. My boxing taught me how to follow a regime. I've got that power in me: if I want to. I went through the twelve step program. You have to take a right good look at yourself. Because I know what my defects of character are – that's what they call them - I can see where things'll lead. Anger, self-pity – something can happen and it's like a doomsday scenario.

What I say to people struggling now is, no matter what, don't use. Hang in. Go to your bed. For me, the power of example is dead strong. That's where my higher power is. I've had to make amends with the wreckage of my past.

I've come here to Whiteinch so I'm as far away from Possilpark as possible. I keep clean company. That's what you need to do. If I hang about a pub long enough I'll say, hey gie me one of those! I know what I'm like. At times I've repeated the same mistakes expecting different results and I've had to pull myself back again.

I got my place here in 2002. That's when my son came back to stay with me so I'm a single parent now. It's a responsibility I've had to fight for.

The boxing club's amazing. We've been running it for about nine months. It's mixed – boys and lassies, from five to thirty year old. Last week we had over forty people there. We start off with rounds of skipping, then a routine of exercises. Then we do padwork with four trainers. We teach them techniques; let them get into controlled aggression, forcing them to work. I say, you're no here to fight, you're here to box. Fighting's a mess – all elbows and arms and heids. It's trying to get them to box, keep your hands up, rather than the square go stuff. Now we've got more facilities – bags, punch balls, a portable ring. We're getting more popular all the time.

Bobby McDermott runs a boxing club on Monday and Wednesday nights at the Whiteinch Centre.

Recovery meetings of Narcotics Anonymous, Cocaine Anonymous and Al-Anon are all held at The Whiteinch Centre.

5: High Flats

ASYLUM
Joyce Ito

The women's group are having their weekly meeting in the community room of a multi storey block of flats in Glasgow. The mixture of Scottish women and asylum seekers is about half and half. Some of the Pakistani women are wearing colourful traditional dress. The younger ones are dressed casually. An elderly Scottish woman is pouring tea and coffee and handing out biscuits. Some of the women are threading beads to make necklaces and bracelets. Two women are unravelling a pile of wool into neat balls. A journalist is taking down is taking notes for a local newspaper.

Delisha:

My sons are doing well in school. Aydin is the top of his class, isn't he?
They miss their papa. He's still in Pakistan but he says not to worry. I have
full refugee status, so I'm allowed to work now but they won't recognise my
degree here. I can speak seven languages but I can't find a job.

Carrie Ann:

I think it's nice having the asylum seekers here. Mrs Amin invited us to
her's for Christmas dinner and we had curry as well as turkey. It was nothing
like the curry you get from the takeaway.

Jazeera:

I came on my own with the children. It was just too dangerous at
home. We lived near the border with Afghanistan. My mother-in-law wasn't
well enough to travel so my husband couldn't leave her but he made us go.
He joined us when she died but now they won't give him refugee status. He's
still an asylum seeker. That means he can't work. He worked long hours in
Pakistan. Now he just sits and stares at the wall.

70

Diane:

Jazeera brings beads and we make jewellery. The asylum seeker weans go to Highland dancing classes at the Community Centre. My weans tried to learn their dances for the festival but they kept falling over.

Shenaz:

I got a job because I speak good English. My husband takes the children to school and makes their meals, helps them with homework. He does it but he feels ashamed. He was a different man before. Now he's so angry. He never drank until we came here. He feels he let his family down because he left his sisters back home. We have to lie when we phone home. I got a promotion but I'm afraid to tell him.

Diane:

Gurpreet was that shocked when she got here. The Home Office man asked if she was married and she's standing there with her three boys and she's not sure if he's having a laugh or insulting her or what. She'd never met a single parent before. Me and Gurpreet are friends. Her boys play with mine. She says her Mammy and Daddy wouldn't let her speak to me in Pakistan cause I've not married ma weans's Da. Things is different here. Not that many people get married any more and most of the ones that do get divorced. Gurpreet says there isn't any divorce where she comes from.

Farida:

The doctor gave me pills for depression. I cannot settle here. I miss Pakistan. People say I have to get used to it and stop crying like a baby but I am not able to stop. How would you feel if you were dropped in the middle of Peshwar? The other asylum seekers are still strangers; hardly anyone speaks the same language as me. People think we are all best friends. Because I have no children I will never get refugee status. It will just go on and on. I can't seem to learn English. My mind is slower here. It must be the cold. I take the pills every day but I wish I had never come.

Mrs McColl:

I was raging about it. I even went to the polis to say he was missing. They said he went home. What home is that I says. Amir's home is next door to mine. Flat 205. That's Amir's home I says, that's where his clothes is. That's where his picture of his mum is, up there on his mantelpiece. We can't help you madam, they said. It's pure criminal, man, that Home Office. They never let him say cheerio or pack his stuff or nothing. I'm ashamed of it, even though it was nothing to do with me. They've stopped the dawn raids now. Cause we got it in the papers. Scaring people out their wits and bundling them in vans at five in the morning, weans in their pyjamas. We had lookouts watching for the Home Office vans and a safe house, just an empty flat with some old chairs and stuff. They were that scared. I don't care what anyone says. It isni right, it just isni right.

ANURA
Sarah Ward

Anura was standing on the balcony taking down washing before she left for work when she heard they had caught Prabhakaran. She went inside to turn up the volume on the television, watching *End of Tamil Tigers* flash over the screen. She sat down. Crowds surged through the dark streets of Columbo, waving banners and clambering onto shoulders and walls to cheer. A journalist clung to the arm of a young man. *How does it feel to see the end of the LTTE?* At first she couldn't hear his reply, only the movement of his lips. The picture crackled and his voice returned... *in fear of suicide bombers. Our children have grown up in the shadow of the Black Tigers. Now we can walk down the streets in safety.*

She looked at her watch: it would be after nine in Sri Lanka. Nihal would be celebrating with his sister's family. The boys hadn't seen their father for six years. They spoke on the phone, but the boys were Scottish now. The man they spoke to didn't know their friends or the streets where they played, the television programmes or the playstation. Samanjan still said, I miss you, Daddy, at the end of the call, but Malik was distant and uncomfortable, and kept the conversation brief. The house was quiet with the boys at school. She stood and brought in the pile of folded dry clothes for ironing.

Rain had streaked the aeroplane windows the night they touched down at Heathrow and the yellow airport lights spilled across the puddles as the plane taxied towards the terminal. Inside they sat in a busy waiting room under the buzz of strip lights. She completed papers while the boys ate curled cheese sandwiches from a steel tray on the steward's counter.

Where are we going? she asked at the desk.

Coach D, he said. Glasgow.

We were told we would stay in London, she said.

You're being sent where the housing is available.

But we have friends in London.

Same as everybody. Nothing I can do, I'm afraid.

How far to Glasgow?

Eight hours. The Dispersal Officer will advise you on board the coach.

Eight more hours. The boys were already worn out. Samanjan had woken on the plane, crying for his dad. She walked back to the bench where they were waiting.

We have a house, she said, but it's in another city. We have a bus journey to get there.

What city? asked Malik. You said London.

I thought London, she said. But they have changed their minds. Now they say Glasgow.

Where is Glasgow? said Samanjan.

In the north, she said. She stroked his head. You can sleep some more, and when you wake, we'll be there.

The coach left towards midnight. It was full of families, some from their flight. Malik sat in the seat in front, Samanjan lay with his head in her lap. The bus was chilly so she covered him with her shawl. The dispersal officer moved up and down the aisle with his clipboard. British people looked like they did at home: shiny, red-faced and official. Anura had done well at school. Her English was good and she had passed her exams and gone on to secretarial studies. In Columbo she was lucky, she had a good job. Here she wouldn't be allowed to work, not for the moment at least. But the boys would be safe and she could send them to school without fearing she might not see them again. She leant her head against the window with the lights of passing cars flashing over her eyelids.

She had woken to a dawn sky. They passed a metal sculpture of a horse, then a sign on a storage vat that said *Glasgow Smiles Better*. She shook Samanjan awake.

This is the place, she said.

He peered out from under his long eyelashes at the grey morning. I want Dad to come, he said.

He can't leave the shop, she said. If he leaves, we'll lose our money. When things are calmer, then he'll come.

But things didn't get calmer; they got worse. Nihal's brother disappeared. Anura argued with Nihal on the phone, urging him not to travel to the north to look for Dileep.

They will take you as well, she said. Then our sons won't have a father or an uncle.

They spent the first Christmas with their Polish neighbours. Anura made a mild curry and Mrs Bisek brought sausage and pickles. Malik and Andrei Bisek spent the afternoon playing games on the old computer Anura had been given by the Refugee Council. When she woke the next day, she lay in bed and smiled because they had made some friends. She sat down with her tea to hear the morning news. Aerial pictures were showing villages and towns submerged underwater. Tsunami. She had never heard the word before. She couldn't reach Nihal for five days because the phone lines were jammed. When he finally got through, his voice sounded different.

Columbo is full of people with nothing, he said. Everyone has lost something. Or someone.

When Anura enquired about applying for asylum status for Nihal, she was told her husband was not a priority. Since he has an income and lives in the capital, we do not regard him as being at significant risk, said the letter. She crumpled the paper and tossed it in the bin then phoned Nihal. He didn't much want to discuss it, and told her instead of the progress he'd made in the shop with the supplies coming through at last. She wouldn't recognise the place.

I think you're going to like it a lot, he said. There is less fighting now. It's safer here, and they are rebuilding all the time. Next year would be a good time to come back.

Malik will start secondary next year, Nihal, she'd said. The boys will get a good education here. Maybe after that.

Anura switched off the TV and went out to the balcony. The blocks of flats were soft brown like sugar and the trees shuffled in the breeze. From here she could see the low single story block of the health centre where she had worked as a receptionist since they had been granted leave to remain, three years ago. She'd promised the boys a holiday before Malik started university and Samanjan at secondary school. When she'd suggested Sri Lanka, Malik had screwed his nose up.

That's not a holiday, Mum. If you go to Sri Lanka, I'm not coming. What about Spain? Andrei went there last year; he said it was brilliant.

But what about your father?

He shrugged. What am I going to talk about for two whole weeks? He'll want me to work in the shop; he'll try to make me stay. I don't want to run a shop in Columbo, I want to be a computer programmer. Please Mum, let's go somewhere fun, just for us.

Malik showed her how to book online. Glasgow to Malaga return. Adult,one; Children, two. Malik hadn't stopped smiling since.

Anura lifted down her coat ready for work. As she reached her arms into the sleeves the phone began to ring. She stood and considered her reflection. She was hopeless at keeping secrets. She buttoned methodically while the phone rang on then lifted her bag and stepped onto the landing, clicking the door behind her. When she paused at the door she heard only silence.

HIGH FLATS
Liam Doherty (age 10)

How did the
builders make it so
high? Must be
scary up
there but
brilliant to live at the
top, like you're
touching the sky
watching tiny
cars, way
down
below.

RECLAD
Neil Robertson

Standing at the end of the
catwalk, this draughty skinny
tower block with tailor-fitted
overcoat will welcome future
winters like a cashmere goat.
New model, beautifully shown;
thicker skin wrapped over
raggled bone.

6: Park

FOSSIL GROVE
AN UNDERCOVER R.I.G.S.
Etta Dunn

Sounds like an oil well
in disguise
spying on maritime activity.
But no, it's a Regionally
Important Geological Site.
The first one in the world housed.

Whiteinch, a tourist attraction?
Fancy that!
Who'd have thought?
Stumps of Giant Clubmosses
as they once grew.
over three hundred million years ago.

Arborescent lycopods,
roots spread out
like two-toed wolves.
A fallen trunk, once support
for an evergreen canopy
trapping solar energy.

Here, whinstone slurry
flooded plants
creating casts of a past life.
Elsewhere wind-fallen forests
compacted into coal seams
or formed oil reserves.

Chemical energy from
heat and light
in the Carboniferous period,
re-cycled to heat and light
our homes and power industry.
The wealth of a nation...

IN ALL WEATHERS
Robert McDermott

The alarm startles me. As I swing my legs ooti the bed, I peek oot the windi to see the sun beams lighting up the outside world. The sky's clear. It's a wonderful mornin. I shout Marco.

'Get up, it's eight o'clock, get washed, brush yer teeth, come oan son, come oan. We've nae time to waste, you'll be late for school.'

As the wee man's in the bog gettin spruced up I'm gettin my camera equipment ready and thinking it's gonni be a good day today. It's autumn. The colours are fantastic this time of year.

So the wean's off to school and I'm off to the park, hoping to see some wildlife. I passes the fossil grove wi the prehistoric deid trees, but I like takin photies of living things. I'll walk round, I thinks to maself, see if I can see the wee wren I took a picture of in the spring. It was in and out its nest feedin its young yins, bringin up its wee family. Nae luck, it's moved on, no even a trace of the nest. Anyway, well, I'm just gonni go up to the duck pond where they said a kingfisher made an appearance last month.

You'd think it was a summer's day the way the sun's splittin the sky, but it's freezin. The weans are all in school; the flowers are finished till next year. The trees are bare, they look nearly as deid as the fossil grove ones. Winter's comin fast. The park's that quiet. It feels like the whole place is mine to enjoy to maself. It doesni matter when I go to the park, I always enjoy it, even in the snow or the howling wind and rain.

The park's been here since before I was born, but I never went. It's no the park that's changed. It's me. Its took me fifty years to get in tune wi nature. I must've been a right bampot and what a waster, but I don't waste ma time any more.

I'm never out the park. In all weathers. I love it.

THE JOYFUL SWINGS
Chantelle Dunlop (age 9), Lauren Dobbie (age 9), Aimee Jade Sawers (age 9), Patrick Whittam (age 9), and Lara Martin (age 10)

'What did you do at school today, Patrick?' said Mum.

'Good things,' I said, running out the door.

There was a fair at the Whiteinch Park and I was off to meet my friends as fast as I could. When I got there they were arguing.

'There's an invisible fish in the pond. If you give him a coin you can make a wish,' said Lara.

'But we've only got money for ice cream and rides,' said Chantelle.

'A penny each and we'll make one wish to the magic fish,' said Lauren.

'Okay,' I said, putting my penny in. 'Let's wish for a magic fair.'

We all shut our eyes and wished.

When we opened them the music was playing and it all sounded amazing fun. We raced to the funfair. There was a sign said THE JOYFUL SWINGS and we all climbed on the ride. It went round and round and faster and faster until it took us to magic place. Then it wasn't so fun. We could see ghosts flying round beside us and it was lonely and creepy and you could just hear the noise of the machines. I felt dizzy and sick and afraid and wanted to get off the ride. Eventually the ride slowed down and let us off.

There was a policeman on a black and white horse and we told him what happened.

'I don't know what ride you mean,' he said.

'THE JOYFUL SWINGS,' Aimee said. 'It's up there in big letters.'

But when we looked round there was only the chute and the rounda-bout and the climbing frame. We petted the horse and ate ice cream and nobody wanted to make any more wishes.

'What did you do in the park, Patrick?' said Mum.

'Fun things,' I said.

GROWING UP IN WHITEINCH
D. McInnes

My earliest childhood recollection was of noise: riveters and calker's pneumatic hammers that reverberated through the air from steel hulls under construction; the trams rattled and rumbled; the 'red buses' added to the cacophony as their tyres ran at speed over the cobbled road. It was the late 1940s and the shipbuilders worked 24/7 to replace the ships lost in the war. There were six major shipbuilders within a half-mile radius of our top floor 'room and kitchen' in Whiteinch. I watched the bright flashes in the night sky as the electric welders would strike their arcs constructing a new ship.

I don't ever recall a time when my mother didn't go out to work. During the day she cleaned for some toff who lived up on Southbrae Drive and twice a week she worked evenings cleaning business premises. My father worked a fifty-two hour week in the shipyards as a 'rid leeder' coating the raw steel with highly toxic paint called red lead. I always remember my dad getting us up at five o'clock on Christmas morning so we could open our presents before he left for work.

With both parents working long hours I was often left in the care of my sister who was six years older than me. Today social services would have something to say, but then it was a tight knit little community; of the twelve families living up our close we were directly related to four and the rest were related to each other or had family very nearby. We had five or six extra mothers, any one of whom would clip us round the ear hole if we were cheeky or put themselves in danger to protect us from harm. They also gave us jeelly-pieces wrapped in greaseproof paper which they would throw from an upstairs window to supply our dietary needs. The one thing drummed into us as children was our name and address: when we had that off by heart we could run wild in the backcourts with the rest of the local kids.

My fascination for the pond in Victoria Park often led me to disobey the cardinal rule never to leave the backcourt. More than once I was escorted home dripping wet after falling in and being fished out. The few whacks I got across my backside for disobeying never seemed stop me and in the end my worried mum and dad sent me for swimming lessons. I started in the wee pool at Whiteinch baths; soon I could swim a whole length of it without any floats and I was allowed into the big pool. I loved swimming so much I was soon there five times a week.

In those days the Whiteinch baths had a steamy. Local women would turn up with a pram loaded with the week's washing. If you helped them up the stairs you'd be rewarded with a penny or two; as soon as I'd earned my 3p entrance fee I was into the pool. I was at the swimming so often I knew all the attendants by name and they would let me stretch my half hour session to an hour if it was quiet. On a Saturday morning I could usually manage from 9am to lunchtime before being kicked out.

On Saturdays we went to our local cinema and then played in Victoria Park. The pond was the Atlantic Ocean, the old red ash football field was the Sahara Desert and the grass was the prairie where Roy Rodgers and Tex Ritter did battle with the redskins.

The model yacht sailing regattas that were held on the Victoria Park pond fascinated me. Just round the corner from our house was Todd's newsagent where Terry lived; he was in his twenties and I was eight. He raced a class 'A' yacht in the regattas; it was about two metres long and had a huge sail which would carry it at a rate of knots across the pond. Terry entrusted me with the pole used to turn the boats around and prevent them from damage if they collided with the bank; I had to turn them the proper way or it would be a foul and the boat would be disqualified. The boats were that fast it took a person running along each side of the pond to do it.

In the winter of 1953, when I was nine, my parents received word that we had been allocated a new house in a place called Drumchapel. The family went the following Sunday to see the proposed site of the new house. After boarding a number 15 bus to its terminus on Great Western Road and then trekking for miles up a farm track up to our knees in mud and snow I got my first sight of Drumchapel, which took my breath away. Here was a place for some new adventures.

LEGACY
Kathy Caldwell

The Fossil Grove is cold as you go in because the trees have turned to stone. They're millions of years old. I'd love to walk over it but you can't do that. They were discovered by mistake many years ago: it's in the history books. It's all grey. To see it in its best light you've to go on a sunny day. There's a viewing platform. These days they've got information up.

They used to have goldfish in the pond. Beautiful lily pads as well. Before they put that road running through it, through Balshagary. There's a bench in there to Mrs Scott. We thought about getting a bench in there for Sandy, my husband. There's a lot of benches right round the park dedicated to the memory of loved ones who used to go there and enjoy it. I was in the park recently with Jack, in his pram. I saw the heron there. It always comes back.

COMMUNISM IN WHITEINCH AND CHILE
Barry Docherty

In 1974 I was a painter in Yarrows shipyard. We were up on scaffolds, cleaning and priming and painting coat after coat of paint on the boats. It was
backbreaking work and the fumes would have Health and Safety closing the
place down today. I was a Red Clydesider, a Communist, and the painters'
shop steward. The guys called me Black Cloud when they were friendly and
Charlie Manson when they'd had enough. I didn't do much painting.

In Chile, General Pinochet, a fascist funded and supported by the
CIA, had overthrown Salvador Allende's democratically elected socialist
government. I spent my spare time helping traumatised Chilean refugees
re-home in Scotland. I would welcome them, hug the weans and find them
second hand furniture. I had no Spanish and they didn't speak a word of
English; many were families with very young children. One was a solitary
sixteen-year old girl with a baby strapped to her hip; she must have been a
serious threat to the Chilean government. In the yards we were building three
frigates for Chile's new fascist regime. It made my blood boil to be painting
Pinochet's warships.

The guys in the yard listened when they were feeling cheerful, ignored
me when they'd had enough. They tolerated my lectures, built ships while
I studied Lenin and Marx in the bothy, and shook their heads at my ravings
about anarcho-syndicalism and Euro communism. They were good guys;
they just wanted to collect their wages and go home. My instructions were to
get them to boycott work on Pinochet's ships. I called a meeting in the yard
to carry the Party line.

'Brothers, we can't work on this ship. Fascists have overthrown the
democratically elected government of Chile. Ordinary men like us have been
thrown out of their jobs and homes for their political beliefs. They've been
robbed. Activists have been tortured and murdered. We must act against
General Pinochet. We are men of integrity. We will not build warships for
them. Are you with me brothers?'

'What has things like that got to do with me, Black Cloud? I don't

know anything about Chile, and I don't want to know anything about it. It's no ma job to fix the world.'

'Do you think these guys from Chile give a damn about us? Do you think they would go on strike to save our arses?'

'Listen, son, you want me to go home to my wife and five weans, five weeks afore the fair, and tell them am no getting paid? I'm on strike in solidarity with some guys I've never clapped eyes on from a country I've never heard of. Aye right. Haud me back.'

Big John was one of the better ones. Intelligent and decent, he was a good family man, someone who could look after himself but never took liberties. John thought of himself as a good trade unionist, a left winger who dealt in common sense rather than anything ideological. I knew that if I couldn't shift him that we'd no chance of winning the vote to boycott work on the frigates for Pinochet's Chile.

But right now, at ten past eight in the morning with the rain pissing down and my head like a washing machine, Chile was the least of my worries. Last night had been a nightmare. A knock on the door around nine o'clock brought eight drunken, screaming madmen bursting into the lobby. Gangster Number 1 swatted me to one side, while another two pinned me by the throat against the wall, demanding to know where the gun was. Number 1's iron grip on my throat and his screaming hostility was affecting me slightly less than his boozy breath and the taste of his spit in my mouth.

'Where is it ya commie, fenian bastard? Tell us now. Tell that cow of yours to show us where it is. Right fuckin now boy. Or we will rip your head off. And she'll wish she had never clapped eyes on you.'

I managed to hold it together enough to see my wife shaking, eyes popping, in deep shock. She pleaded with the leader to be allowed to go to the toilet.

'You gonny pish yer knickers hen? Give the boys a treat? Tell yer man to give us the gun and you can pish till your wee heart's content. Otherwise, let's see it for the boys. Know what I mean honey?'

I knew that Marjie would be in trouble if I didn't pipe up fast. I begged them to let her use the toilet and I would give them what they wanted.

'Right bawheid, gun. Now!'

'Look, mate,' I said, playing for time, 'I don't know anything about any gun, and you canny barge into peoples houses threatening to kill them. That's serious stuff: Who are you?'

'Just batter him,' said the one with the soft hat and collar and tie. 'We've wasted enough time. Stop messing about and we can get home early.'

'Trust me sunshine,' said Number 1, 'we can ruin your life. We can put you in hospital, get you sacked with a guarantee you'll never work again. He pushed his face into mine. Or we can, eh, disappear you. Just like that.'

If Marjie hadn't emerged from the toilet screaming the place down at precisely that moment, I suspect I would have been shown how serious my visitors were.

'We're Special Branch,' he hissed, 'we answer to no one. I promise you, we will find the gun. We will tear this place apart to get it.'

'Wire in, I said. If you find a gun, you're welcome to it.

They turned the house upside down. No gun.

'Right guys, nothing doing, arsehole here doesn't have the bottle. We're out of here.' My speech about my human rights was interrupted by a sledgehammer blow from behind to the back of my head, which sent me crashing face first to the floor where I burst my nose on the new carpet tiles Marjie's mum had just paid for.

Morning. Late again for the quarter to eight whistle that started the day-shift in the yard. My mate Jimmy would risk his job and the security of his family to stamp my card again. I knew that, but I also knew that management were paying me very close attention. They wanted me out of there fast. As I skulked along South Street looking for a spot to jump the wall, I heard the voice of Jack Askey, Communist Party industrial organiser for Scotland:

'No discipline, no dignity of labour, no humility, poor timekeeper, poor skills as a tradesman. And you're a womaniser. You prefer whisky to work. Still, you're not daft, you can talk, and you can definitely swing this vote for the boycott if you put your mind to it. Question is, will you, can you?

Or are you going to be sacked for something stupid before the big meeting? It's good communists we need.'

I could handle the special branch, handle the verbal and physical attacks from workmates and others, handle the distress my being in the party caused my Irish catholic family, handle being blacklisted from work. But I couldn't cope with getting to work on time, couldn't do a day's work for a day's pay, couldn't respect anyone or anything. Jack Askey was right. A disciplined hero of labour I was not.

General Pinochet got his three warships and he prospered in Chile with the support of the United States and the CIA. He was a friend of Margaret Thatcher's and was welcomed in Great Britain by the Tory government. To their everlasting shame, the Scottish football team played football in the Santiago stadium where Pinochet had tortured and murdered hundreds of Chilean democrats. In the end Pinochet was charged and found guilty of war crimes, but he evaded imprisonment by claiming to suffer from Alzheimer's disease and died a free and very rich man aged 91. His family inherited millions of pounds, thought to be misappropriated public funds. Thousands of missing Chilean democrats and socialists remain unaccounted for to this day.

CRANE
Jay Cherrie (age 10)

I heard the crane came from China on a boat.
It moves when I'm not looking.
> Builds
> Lifts
> Makes
> ships by the
> Clyde.
> Towers above,
> watches
> them sail
> away.

From 'PLACES WHERE PEOPLE LIVE'
Number One: A GLASGOW SKIPPER
Neil Mackay

There's a regulatory light -
no wait, don't go -
that just flows
off the old granary.
Follow it - like, way down there -
as it cuts between the casino
and the flats,
and it comes to where
the spot
and the light
just give up and
just don't care.
But there are houses in the bits
between the lights
not even near.

Or rather, not houses, just locations,
where other people live
who struggle with
life's syncopation.

Walk in the door,
if this is a place that has a door,
and there's a
mattress on the floor
laid out in proper bedroom style -
a place that folk could live in
for a while.

Some books, candles all succumbed
and a little tin
that people really -
actually's the word -
drink from.

A cabin freely left years before
by builders wearing quiffs.
She's even put some curtains up
and a print -
a bear gone mad, a bit skew-wiff,
with a tiger chasing after it.
Cellotape squint.

That makes it homely when it's dark.

Outside
leaned against
a fence
is her boy
called
Mark.

THE COLINA
D. Laverie

Peter shook his head, listening to the austere quiet, broken by the occasional squawking of a gull over King George V docks. He stood east of the defunct Braehead Power Station and directly south across the river from Whiteinch, looking at what was left of the once-famous shipyard of Barclay Curle. As if hypnotised, his thoughts drew him back to the time when the Glasgow branch of the British Shipping Federation employed thousands of Glaswegian seamen. He had joined a ship in 1960 at Meadowside Quay; the vessel was the MV Colina owned by Donaldson Line, recently built in Aberdeen, preparing for its maiden voyage. Peter was employed as an able-bodied seaman but was only to complete one return trip on the ship across the Atlantic to the North American coast.

In those days, the officers did not mix with the crew. Visitors and agents from the ports into which the Colina sailed came onboard to be wined and dined by the Captain and his officers. The crew were anonymous. It was this social division that caused him to leave the ship; there was no other reason.

It was by chance that Peter had met the owner of a British coaster that was to be delivered within the month to Newfoundland. He took the name of the company and when he arrived back in Glasgow, he called and asked to be a member of the crew. He was told to get down to London where the ship lay, as it would be sailing in a few days. With the help of the ship's owner, Peter gradually built a new life in Canada, continuing to work on the same ship until it was eventually sold again. Within a few years he married and his wife encouraged him to apply to Canadian Nautical College where he gained qualifications to be a deck officer on a Home Trade vessel. For the moment, he was employed on an anchor-handling vessel towing icebergs, amongst the many duties in the heavy cold Western Atlantic Ocean, in what was Canada's first attempt at drilling offshore for oil. After a few years, he improved his qualifications again, and his yearning for deep-sea sailing was rewarded when he was sent to join a vessel trading in the West Indies from Kingston, Jamaica.

As he climbed the accommodation ladder of the ship, Crewman

Andrew Crosbie, took his baggage and directed him to the captain's office. Peter was introduced to the Chief Engineer, and passed over his documents and seaman's discharge book to the captain for inspection. He was aware that the Captain was looking at him rather strangely, only indicating that Peter should take a seat as he flipped through his discharge book. Suddenly, with a roar that stunned Peter into silence, the captain bawled in a broad Glaswegian, 'Peter Piper! I'll be damned The Colina! Don't you remember? I was third officer on the maiden voyage and you were on my watch!'

'Not really', said Peter, 'all Glaswegians look the same to me.'

The men broke into laughter and the captain told him that the ship was the old Colina, belonging to Donaldson Line, bought and lengthened at Barclay Curle's yard in 1966. This man, whom Peter had considered a social enemy in the past, became firm friends even when they parted. They met on numerous occasions, often in strange circumstances and places. He smiled happily at the fond memories. His reverie was broken by a security man calling out, 'Hey Jimmy! Do you know this is private property and no-one is allowed in here?'

In 1990, Peter returned home to Glasgow, which he had not seen for twenty-three years. His time during that period had been spent working on Canadian shipping. His reason for returning was twofold: he needed to continue to work, and he wanted to avoid the Canadian winter. Although Canada has laws against age discrimination, work at sea was becoming more difficult to obtain due to age, even though he was only fifty years old. But he had become aware that there was a shortage of officers in the British merchant navy and this was why he had returned.

Having safely landed at Heathrow, he picked up a newspaper and read the story of a man who had not been so fortunate. The day before, a cold wintry day in Glasgow, a body had impacted in Victoria Park. One flip-flop was still attached to a dismembered frozen foot, which lay a metre away. Newspaper reports stated that there was no doubt he had departed an aircraft when the aircrew had lowered the wheels in preparation for landing; most likely he had been dead from hyperthermia long before he fell from the wheelbase. The man was listed as unknown origin, probably Asian, and an illegal entrant. He had managed to avoid detection at the airport he came from, but sadly knew nothing of the atmospheric conditions at 32,000 feet above the ground.

Peter arrived home to find that the city had changed dramatically, all along the river banks. His home was gone. The motorway crossed the stark river, bleak with the absence of ships and movement on the docksides. There were no shipyards left now in Whiteinch, and no trains. The only vessel using the river was the Yoker to Renfrew ferry from which he had just disembarked at Renfrew. The cold sunny weather emphasized the decline of the ferry landing. Glasgow was no longer dependent on shipping and heavy engineering, and was now struggling to understand the new service and tourism sectors. Tradesmen, dockers and labourers, many from generations of families who had given a lifetime to their field of work, could not and would not diversify. Parts of the city had become a stagnant pool of indifference, breeding apathy, and it showed on the streets. Boarded-up shops invited graffiti. Run-down movie theatres, a lack of public swimming pools and play areas for sports, gave the impression of a listless crime-ridden neglected city. Glasgow now looked like one of the many American city ghettos he had seen on his travels.

Those days seem aeons ago to Peter, who often felt as though he was invisible. He wondered what the future held for the young; for him, progress now meant a disappearing past. He imagined his furniture and other belongings thrown onto the street on his demise. But life for new generations would continue bringing new ideas and fresh thoughts. Peter still lived in Whiteinch, now transformed by the new community centre which has become a focal point for local people. He wondered who amongst today's young people would create a bright new future, bringing pride to their community?

THE DUMP
Andrew Kelly (age 9)

I wonder why
people throw out all that
stuff? Where does it
go? It makes me feel
sad when it
smells so bad. Turns this
place into a
dump.

WHITE MR INCH
Annabel Drysdale

Way out west in the flow of the river
lay an isle full of riches: pieces of silver
were strewn over the ground but no-one could
could reach it without being drowned.
For the island was under a terrible curse
that punished those looking to line their purse.

On each bank lived a clan with a claim to the space
where the silver was lying all over the place.
A bald-headed preacher interrupted their fight
to call for a truce to be reached by that night.
But none could agree; so to teach them a lesson
He placed his worst curse on the island between them:

'Touch the silver that's there and you'll be turned to dust;
A shared use of land by both clans is a must.
Reach agreement on how you will share the wealth out
Or the island will sink and you'll be left with nowt!'

The clan on the left were the Metrics, so tall!
But the ones on the right, the Imperials, were small.
Together they'd lived on the banks of The Slosh,
for decades they'd fought, but neither would cross
to the isle in the middle to see was it true,
that touching the silver made sand out of you.

The Imperials herded their cattle and sheep
and lived on a diet of mutton and beef.
The Metrics kept an orchard where grew all things green
like lettuces, cucumber, tomatoes and beans.

In the house on the right, Mr Inch did reside
and being quite quiet, he tended to hide
inside the front room that was barren and bare.
Till one day, came crashing onto his chair
a keyboard and computer, complete with a mouse
as though someone knew what he'd lacked in his house!

So onto the web: Mr Inch found a way
to study and read and learn more day by day.
He turned himself into the brain of his clan;
By reading and watching he could understand
that sitting about on his bum all day long
was a waste of his life, and so terribly wrong.
Watching football and rugby he knew bit by bit
Sport would get him outside and make his body real fit!

Unknown to our friend, that same day from the sky
a TV landed on Mr Metre's home baked pie!
'Oh my!' Metre shrieked, 'What's the meaning of this?'
'A television? Wow! What a fabulous gift!
I can sit on the sofa and be entertained
And stay dry on the nights when it heavily rains!'

So he sat and he watched and his bum grew in size
because he stopped with the gardening and the making fine pies.
In a moment of madness, he leaped in despair
(Then had to try harder since he stuck in the chair!)
'I'm getting so fat that I need to play sport
outside with my friends; that's a fabulous thought!'

With a turnip plucked out of his vegetable plot
He chased it around like he'd seen on the box.
The goal posts he used were the trunks of two trees
And he managed to score with the greatest of ease.

Then he spied, on the other bank, a sight to behold
Mr Inch running round with a ball, but no goals.
His posts were two sheep which wandered at will
where the green grass was tasty, so were never still.
To score even once seemed to be such a chore;
then he saw across the bank Mr Metre score more
than he'd seen in a game with Ronaldo or Becks!
With penalty shots and some great corner kicks.

Quite in awe, Mr Inch looked across at his foe
And wondered if he could be granted a go?
It was more fun to play against a real person
Than playing alone with a sheep – that's for certain!
But to speak to THAT man was against the clan's orders.
He could do nothing more but then Metre looked over
and saw that his foe had the same thoughts as him
Playing footie together would make it more challenging!

Misters Metre and Inch knew what had to be done:
In both of their minds a new plan was begun.
Their ancient feud would now be put to rest
And the island between them made into the best
place for both clans to transform lazy bums.
Yes, a pitch would be built - a great giant stadium!

Then down from the sky, in a big floating bubble
Descended the preacher; he came on the double.
With a swish of his wand and an 'Abracadabra!'
the curse of the island vanished forever!
So happy was he to tell both of the clans
That as long as it was built with everyone's hands
The pitch would be sacred and a safe place to play
With the Imperials and Metrics forever okay!

So the folks were ecstatic and declared with much glee
That the first game was planned for Saturday at three.
The whistle was blown and the game had begun
Cheers rang through the stadium, fans having fun.
With the teams in formation on the pitch 4 – 4 - 2
The coin tossed, the ball dropped, the whistle blew...

THE LAST OF THE FREE
'M'

What you are about to read will be easily passed off as fantasy. The race of people from 2010 may be incapable of understanding the events. I do not ask that you believe.

It started in Whiteinch, in July, 2001. My grandfather had just passed away and my grandmother was clearing out his belongings. She came across a small wooden box. It was a box she had seen many times before. She knew a key for it hung in the closet. She put it in the lock. Click. It opened. What she saw meant nothing to her but that click changed my life forever. She swung the lid open and focused on a bunch of old coins and a very old looking knife. She placed the box to the side. My Grandfather had left it to me.

That Saturday morning the box lay on my Grandmother's kitchen table waiting for me. I opened it. The knife lay on the coins: a lock knife. I took it out, rested it on the window ledge and inspected the coins: nothing special, a few silver dollars and a copper coin. The copper one was not a normal coin. On one side it said 'THEY RECIEVED EVERY MAN A PENNY.' It had a small circle within the centre and within that circle a triangle. Around that it had the letters TKSHTWSS. On the other side it had a name and the word LODGE and CLYDE with a thistle. These all meant something, but what?

Later that night I got home and turned on my computer. My grandmother knew nothing about old coins, but I had the advantage of being able use the internet. I found out that the copper coin was from the not so secret society, The Masons.

The next day I was at my grandmother's again to clear some things out. She went out to the shops and I found myself staring out over the Clyde, watching a ship pass. The coin was in my hand. I missed my grandfather; I wasn't the only one.

A knocking at the door caught my attention. I answered it and a young man stood, looking upset, saying he was an old friend of my grandfather's. He must have been twenty five. Strange, I thought, but invited him in. He sat down on the couch and began to speak. He told me that one day, a long time ago, my grandfather helped him: something which had apparently saved his life. He said that because of this he entered my grandfather into a club which he stayed a part of all his life. I threw the coin on the table: The Masons?

'My name is Riley.' he said, standing up and glancing out over the horizon. 'Me and your Grandad planned on going on a trip one day but we never did it. He didn't want to leave your grandmother and I couldn't convince him. He left the box and the coin to you; he wanted you to come on the trip.'

Where did he want me to go? I wasn't going away with some guy I'd just met!

'Where?' I asked

'The future.'

Okay, I thought. This gentleman has obviously just come off the number 9 bus and had too much Buckfast. Then he threw a newspaper on the table. The date on it was 2020. I sat with him for a long time.

'I have a ship under water which is capable of making leaps in time, or rather, leaps in reality. In the universe there are infinite realities; jumps in these realities are possible. Most realities are the same but others have tiny, or even huge, differences. Fate changes direction in time. I wanted to show your Grandfather, but he chose not to go. I want to take you.'

That night we took a motorbike to a shoreline. I have no idea where. We got in a small paddle boat and went out to sea. Riley removed what looked like a mobile phone from his pocket and when it began to beep rapidly he threw himself over the edge. I tried to grab him thinking he was sure to drown, but soon I saw lights come from under me. What I could see approaching from the depths looked more like a gigantic aircraft than a submarine. It came to the surface of the water, a door hissed open and I got in. The craft took off and before I knew it I was heading towards the sky.

A girl was waiting inside with clothes for me; they were plain black except for some very odd looking footwear. She was around my age, just like any normal girl. The craft was like a hospital inside. I went into a small room and got changed behind a curtain. Riley was busy in the cockpit and the girl and I sat talking. Her name was Emily Marshall. She came from Manchester and was a lot older than I thought. She was born in 1805. She called herself 'one of the free.' She eventually called us 'The Last of the Free'. I liked that description.

Emily showed me news flashes from different moments in time:

Scientists find the cell which causes ageing (2051)

The human population is inoculated against ageing and virtually all disease is cured (2055)

The government outlaw ageing (2065)

The Anti-Immortality Regime overthrows the American government (2070)

All out civil war occurs (3000)

Nuclear weapons destroy half the world's population (3010)

A government made infection wipes out a further quarter of the human population. (3015)

I couldn't watch any more. Emily told me Riley had been part of a huge infrastructure of rebels that became time travellers; all of the other rebels were killed in the 3010 bomb blast.

'Why he didn't he just go back and warn them?' I asked.

'Because he might have died too. He had to keep the resistance against the government up at any cost.'

'And now?'

'A group of government soldiers stalk the realities searching for us. If they find us, we're dead. Our job is to change the future so that some events do not occur. We save lives but also fight the world government's plan in making the public a slave nation. We are the last the last of the free.'

I now know the present day as 3582. I've been at this game for a long, long time: longer than I wish to remember. Emily chose to go back to the time she left her family. She managed to steal the antidote to the ageing cell and I watched her die in 1905. She was buried in a Manchester grave yard. I miss her but she made me promise I would never visit her again after her death. She wanted to forget.

Riley and I engraved a message to the people of the United Kingdom on a track, known in 2010 as 'the back road'. It is my favourite place in my grandparent's old home of Whiteinch.

Ye, the last men on earth. The last of the free.

JOHNNY'S FAITH
Stella Capaldi

The tenement door swung shut on the warm June air. Inside the close Johnny kept running, as he had all along South Street. Past the bikes lying against the coal bunker, and Mrs Soutar's pram, and up the stone stairs two at a time, until he reached his Ma's house. He grinned as he looked down at the goldfish in his hands. He couldn't wait to see his Ma's face when he poured it into the fish tank.

In Ma's front room, on her sideboard, was a statue of a boy holding a square glass fish tank. He was about three feet high, pasty like a religious statue of Our Lady from a church or a school. He had painted wavy hair with black lines grooved into it to make it look more real (it had the opposite effect), a pale orange top and brown dungarees. He was barefoot. His eyes were a staring gaudy blue. Johnny loved this statue. It had the serenity of a holy statue looking over them all: it soothed him. Secretly, he had prayed to it when he was sad; it looked over them all. His second eldest brother Frank had bought it for Ma with his first pay packet fifteen years ago.

Johnny let himself in to the narrow hallway. Ma's door was always on the latch. She was a popular woman; local people popped in and out to spend some time with her and get the local gossip.

'Hi everybody, how are all we doing?' shouted Johnny.

In the room and kitchen his three brothers were sitting at the table. He sidled past them to get to his Ma standing between the stove and the sink. She was a well-made woman, robust, selfless. She'd endured everything her four boys went through especially since Pop, their Dad, died ten years ago. They still asked her advice about the family icecream business Pop had left to her. The sons ran it now, but it kept her busy and her mind active.

Johnny and his brothers all looked alike – small and dark, with wavy hair and long Roman noses; the local Scotstoun community often referred them to as the 'Tallies'. They did stand out a bit amongst the fairer, Celtic complexions. They'd inherited Pop's Italian looks.

It was a special day because Johnny had been working on the builidng of the new steam coaster, Marianne, and had been invited to join the maintenance crew, and sail on her maiden voyage to America. It was departing next day; he was so excited, only twenty-two and he couldn't believe the opportunity had come his way. He was glad to be escaping the family ice cream business. His brothers made a decent living out of it and saw Ma alright but they worked long hours. Holidays and travel were out of the question. But they didn't grudge Johnny the chance. Ma had her own thoughts and reservations but she kept them to herself.

Johnny made a quick glance at the statue. His brothers looked up, then at each other, then started to sing:

What will we do with a drunken sailor
What will we do with a drunken sailor
What will we do with a drunken sailor
Early in the morning.

They burst out laughing.

'Ha ha very funny the lot of you,' Johnny said as he kissed Ma's cheek.

'One day to go,' Joe said. 'Still going?'

'Too right I am. I've something here for you Ma. I want you to shut your eyes for a minute.'

He opened the bag and tipped the fish in to the tank.

'Open them Ma.'

Johnny steered her over to the sideboard.

'Aw goodness me,' she gasped, clasping her hands together as Johnny swung her round.

'And you know what that's for? To remind you of me when I'm all at sea. Get it?'

'Johnny, what a thoughtful idea, son,' said Sal. He was the eldest and most serious brother.

'Aye and who'll be left to feed it? That'll be me, no doubt.' said Joe, the closest brother in age to Johnny. 'Ne'er mind though, good shout. I'll do it.'

'What a nice thing to do, son. I can't remember the last time we had any fish in the tank and I don't really know why.'

Johnny took his seat at the table.

'Great stuff and hilarity it may be but let's get some food on the table,' said Sal.

Ma started to put the steaming plates of food in front of her boys. Men leading their own independent lives with families and kids but every Friday they came to Ma's for a family lunch. They started to eat while she fussed around them offering more gravy, more potatoes.

'How am I going to live a year without your gravy, Ma? You'll have to send me some.'

'And exactly how will I manage that, Mister?'

'You could put some in a bottle and set it out to sea labelled Johnny's Ma's best gravy,' said Joe.

'Aye, stick a first class stamp on it. It'll get there in no time,' laughed Johnny.

They joked and ate but there was an edge. No-one said anything.

'So what time are the festivities kicking off then tomorrow?' said Sal.

'The Lord Provost will cut the ribbon and smash the bottle at twelve noon but before that there's a parade. You can watch all the crew mounting the boat so you can all give me a big send off.'

After lunch, Maggie, Johnny's girlfriend, joined them. She was a bubbly, bashful young woman, firmly welcomed into the family by Ma: a compliment in itself. Ma guarded her boys fiercely. Maggie was perfect for Johnny and besotted by him. The three brothers had fun kidding her on about Johnny and how was she going to manage to look after him the way Ma had, him being the baby and all. They were all very fond of her. The wedding had been set for that autumn but after the offer to travel on the ship had come along they had postponed it until the next one. They'd all told him often enough she'd move on in his absence. Or he may find a new love abroad. But she and he were sorted. The statue would see to it. Johnny glanced at the boy and said a short prayer of thanks that Friday. He felt happy and grateful.

The next day Whiteinch celebrated. The sun stayed out. A brass band played while little children marched up and down to the music, balloons were cast into the sky and the crowd cheered. The family was all there to wave Johnny off. He said his goodbyes quickly. He grabbed a brother at a time to him and kissed them then lifted Maggie up, twirled her round and kissed her a long, lingering kiss. He told her he loved her, reminded her to write keeping him up to date on all the wedding plans.

He went to his Ma last. He put his arms around her and as he cuddled her his head rested for a moment on the fur collar of her coat. He snuggled into it. Ma clung to him for a second longer than she should have.

'Bye son,' she said, looking downwards. 'Look after yourself.'

'Thanks for everything Ma. Before you know it I'll be back.' He kissed her soft cheek. 'Look after the fish mind'.

Johnny hurried up the gangplank. Just at the top he turned and waved and did that jokey thing he always did of a daft smile and hunching up his shoulders as if to say what's going on. The family all waved enthusiastically. Then he was out of sight.

The Marianne capsized whilst launching from the shipyard. One hundred and thirty-eight workmen and young men were killed. Johnny was one of them. Johnny's Ma in her grief couldn't bear to keep the statue but gave it to Maggie. Today it stands amongst the dining room shelves of Maggie's great granddaughter. She can't really remember its history but knows it meant an awful lot to her great gran. And she does remember the instruction that whoever has it must always keep a fish in it. And his name should be Johnny.

AN EXCERPT FROM CLYDESIDE MAGAZINE

On the 3rd of July, 1883 Alexander Stephen & Sons, Govan were set to launch a little steamer for the Glasgow & Londonderry Steam Packet Company, Glasgow. The ship was loaded with workers, as was the practice at that time - from young boys to older men, carrying with them their tools, ready to re-start work the minute she was made fast. She was named DAPHNE and she slid into the then putrid waters of the Clyde and almost immediately capsized, trapping the men and boys in the upturned hull. Weighed down by their tools and heavy boots, their struggles only ensured panic and death as they drowned in the filthy water. All told one hundred and twenty-four were killed in the worst ever disaster in the Clyde's shipbuilding history and many, many families in the shipbuilding community were affected as they lost sons, brothers and husbands, on a day that was just routine for them. There is a memorial garden in the Victoria Park dedicated to the unfortunate souls who perished, but their lasting legacy was to ensure that in the future, only the most essential personnel required would be permitted on board a vessel at launch.